Glass Half Empty
Glass Half Full

How Asperger's syndrome has changed my life

Chris Mitchell

P·C·P

Paul Chapman
Publishing

Lucky Duck is more than a publishing house and training agency. George Robinson and Barbara Maines founded the company in the 1980s when they worked together as a head and as a psychologist, developing innovative strategies to support challenging students.

They have an international reputation for their work on bullying, self-esteem, emotional literacy and many other subjects of interest to the world of education.

George and Barbara have set up a regular news-spot on the website at http://www.luckyduck.co.uk/newsAndEvents/viewNewsItems mand information about their training programmes can be found at www.insetdays.com

More details about Lucky Duck can be found at http://www.luckyduck.co.uk/

Visit the website for all our latest publications in our specialist topics

- Emotional Literacy
- Bullying
- Circle Time
- Asperger's Syndrome
- Self-esteem
- Positive Behaviour Management
- Anger Management
- Eating Disorders

ISBN: 1-4129-1162-1

Published by Lucky Duck
Paul Chapman Publishing
A SAGE Publications Company
1 Oliver's Yard
55 City Road
London EC1Y 1SP

SAGE Publications, Inc.
2455 Teller Road
Thousand Oaks, California 91320

SAGE Publications India Pvt Ltd.
B-42, Panchsheel Enclave
Post Box 4109
New Delhi 110 017

www.luckyduck.co.uk

Commissioning Editor: Barbara Maines
Editorial Team: Mel Maines, Sarah Lynch, Wendy Ogden
Cover photo: Jeff Crowe
Designer: Helen Weller

Printed in Great Britain by The Cromwell Press, Trowbridge, Wiltshire.

Printed on paper from sustainable resources.

Contents

'Canada' (2003) shows me with Tara's ASS group in Vancouver. Left to right is Leslie Biensz, Tim Pylupiak, Tara Kimberley Torme, Natalie Beanland and myself.

Foreword

There is always someone who seems a bit 'different' in every school. Someone who is misunderstood, or just does things in his own way, with little or no need to conform to their peers' behaviour. More often than not they become an object of ridicule, bullied and taunted, as if this treatment will somehow make them change and become more acceptable.

Chris Mitchell was this person who was ostracised and targeted because of his different behaviour. His recounting of these times can be difficult to read because we recognise that we may not have helped people like Chris when we were in school. Yet Chris also shares his insight into why he behaved as he did, or at least examines why he couldn't behave as his peers did, and he does not really lay blame.

Chris writes with such insight and humour about his life, that despite my NT status, I really found myself empathizing with his wilderness years, awaiting an answer or reason for his differences. Most teenagers experience a difficult adolescence, when everything seems to be flipped upside down and everything that made sense suddenly doesn't seem that important. For Chris, to have to endure living in a world like this throughout his life, with everyone expecting him to act and behave in a certain way but being unable to, must have been extraordinarily difficult. That Chris not only copes but manages to remain in mainstream schooling and be accepted into university, is inspirational.

The anger that is evident in the first part of this book is also striking. I was worried at times that readers might not be so sympathetic to Chris because of the extent of his anger and frustration, especially when he is looking at his circumstances with the benefit of hindsight. I was also concerned that some people mentioned in the book, especially family members, might be hurt by his comments. I relayed this worry to Chris, who responded:

> I remember that you said when you first read my copy that you felt some of the content might be hurtful to some. None of the content is meant to be hurtful, as the way it is written is about how I felt during certain phases of my life, including what I felt about things around me during particular times.

> Even now, I often talk with my parents and others who played a role in my upbringing about these times, about how I felt about certain aspects of my life (for example, school, playing team sports, university and so on) and they say, 'Oh gosh, did I really do that to you Chris?'

They never meant hurt me in this way either, because they perhaps didn't understand me like many people who know me now do. Just recently, I received a letter from one of my old primary school teachers who was of great help to me when I was that age. She knows that I give talks about Asperger's syndrome and that I sometimes use extracts from school reports in my material, and she said it is interesting for her to see what someone like myself makes of the way teachers interpreted me.

Inclusion is such a topical term now, especially as the support for students with special needs is improving and Chris shows that it is possible to survive in mainstream education without formal support. When additional support is given, real progress can be made. He has really made an effort to transform his life.

I hope that his story will comfort you if you have recently been diagnosed with Asperger's or encourage you if a friend or a family member has been diagnosed. Now that the condition is becoming more understood and recognized, no, one need live in a puzzling haze. There is the chance to be accepted and celebrated for being different.

Sarah Lynch

Author's Note

Being diagnosed with Asperger's syndrome at nearly 20 years old, I feel I have lived two separate lives. For this purpose, I feel that my life story needs two separate sections. Glass Half-Empty is about my life before diagnosis and Glass Half-Full is about my life after diagnosis. The intention of this book is to show how my life has changed since diagnosis, and above all, to recognize the positive aspects of Asperger's syndrome.

Dedication

I would like to dedicate this work to my family for their support since my diagnosis and my friends for all their encouragement.

Chris with his toy train collection as
a child.

Glass Half Empty

1

Introduction:
Childhood Memories

Of all the aspects of my childhood that I remember best, it is my special interests. Some of my early interests also saw me develop obsessive-compulsive tendencies, which at times drove my uncle round the bend!

Stories of obsessions in children and adults with Asperger's syndrome are plentiful, but obsessive-compulsive tendencies in me started at a very early age. Around me, when very young, was my father's model railway collection and my collection of toy cars together with the motor city set that my parents bought me for a birthday present. While my mother was in hospital giving birth to my brother, my grandparents came around to baby-sit me and I remember them giving me a present of a toy car transporter. I loved to arrange all my cars, locomotives and rolling stock in patterns and would have tantrums each time a car was put in the wrong place or the pattern got mixed up.

Early observations

Observations that my parents and grandparents had about me when a pre-school child at playschool and nursery were that I was reluctant to go, and when I did go, I didn't join in games and activities with the other pre-school children. I can remember feeling upset when I first had to attend playschool because I was happy at home playing with my toys. Although there were toys at playschool, they were different to those I had at home, so I didn't understand what their purpose was and they didn't appear to be in any kind of order, often being scattered all over the floor. Whereas some of the other pre-school children around me liked to play together imaginatively with the toys, I couldn't understand what it was about and wanted my own space to play in. At home with my cars and trains, I knew the order they were in and where I could expect to find them.

When three-years-old, my parents moved from Stockton-on-Tees to Washington, Tyne and Wear. This change was apparently very traumatic for me. When seeing all my toy cars being packed into boxes and loaded into a removal van, I at first thought that they were being taken away with the entire contents of the house for good, not realizing that they would be unloaded at our new house. I felt my routine had been dismantled. It took me a long time to settle into our new house in Washington as well as having to get used to a new school.

Slow starter

When starting primary school in Washington in the mid-1980s, I was, academically, a slow developer in most subjects, especially maths. While the other children seemed to be progressing ahead of me, I felt rather left behind. What wasn't noticed back then was that I had a shorter attention span than most other pupils around me and teachers often thought that I was daydreaming. Often, I found myself being blamed for my slow development. The teachers thought that I was holding back the class and my parents kept on at me about Philip, the boy who lived across the road, was two levels ahead of me in reading and many modules ahead of me in maths.

During my primary school years, *Thomas the Tank Engine and Friends* first came on television. The television series provided me with an escape from what I was facing at school. My favourite engine was Henry, because some of the episodes that revolved around him related to how I felt at school, in terms of how I felt left behind. Henry felt that he suffered dreadfully but nobody cared. The other engines said he didn't work hard enough and the Fat Controller said that he was too expensive in terms of all the new parts he needed. Just like it wasn't my fault that I had a short attention span, it wasn't Henry's fault that his firebox was too small to make enough heat required to pull heavy loads, while the other engines could manage as they had larger fireboxes. My parents often became very frustrated with my slow development and they began to monitor me closely, making sure that I did my homework. In some cases, they lost patience with me, which only encouraged me to dislike school more.

Due to my short attention span, I often found myself misinterpreting instructions. For instance, when having to copy words for spelling tests from the blackboard, I only copied about a quarter of them, so when it came to the test, I found that I was having to spell words that I had never heard of. Sometimes, I got lost in terms of knowing what I was supposed to be doing. In one instance, the teacher wrote an outline for a story on the blackboard. Previously, I had been used to having to copy down what was written on the board when learning handwriting, so I assumed that this was what I was supposed to do. This got me into trouble with the teacher as it made me look ignorant, but it was only because I had unintentionally misinterpreted instructions. Other pupils laughed at me for this.

Early interests and first ambitions

Away from school, I found it much easier and far more interesting to find out about different topics through reading. I really enjoyed reading up on information on a variety of topics, particularly relating to history, geography and astronomy through Usborne and Ladybird books. In the classroom though, I felt that I couldn't learn much because I was around other pupils. This made it very difficult for me to focus on whom I was supposed to be paying attention to (the teacher). Quite often though, the topics of interest that I enjoyed to pursue often distracted me from the work or task that I was supposed to be concentrating on, as shown by:

> 'In investigating one aspect of the work, he can easily be sidetracked into other areas as he is attracted by interesting but irrelevant articles in the reference materials etc.' Extract from school report, 1988

Away from the classroom though, spending time by myself in my room reading about some of my favourite topics fed some of my first ambitions. My earliest ambition was to be an astronomer. It all started at Rickleton Primary School during the 1980s, when Mrs Smith, the class teacher, showed a programme entitled *The Boy from Space*. Not only did I thoroughly enjoy the programme, but it also encouraged me to read further into the subject and it wasn't long before I knew all the constellations, the distances from the sun of all the planets and other space related facts.

At home, in our back garden, I liked to observe the night sky, locating where all the stars, planets and constellations were. I found myself drawing images of stars and planets continuously. At first, I copied each of the nine planets to the same size before finding out to how draw them in relation to how large they are compared to each other. I used to like arranging all the planets and stars that I had drawn on the living room floor, like I had previously done with toy cars.

Too much information?

In the classroom, I sometimes found myself in class discussions. In such situations, I often thought that the information I liked to store my brain with would be useful, but what I didn't realise though was that the purpose of such an exercise was to challenge one another's arguments and points of view. Often, I found myself having much information to contribute to class discussions, but when it was challenged, I became very confused:

'In class or area debate, Christopher is an enthusiastic participant, particularly when he has a package of information to deliver. If he has missed the point of the question, and is interrupted, he becomes confused and finds difficulty in collecting his thoughts.' Extract from School Report 1988

Very occasionally, I found that I was able to use some of my knowledge and special interests for group projects. Another of my other childhood obsessions was drawing flags of different nations. I liked finding out about all the different colours and symbols on each flag. I was able to put this interest to good use at the time of the 1986 World Cup.

Previously, I had never paid much attention to football as it was an activity that was played in groups, and I didn't feel as though I had anyone to play with. During the build up to a major sporting event, such as the World Cup, the media often includes huge pullouts or specialist sections often decorated in the flags of the competing nations. For a class project, we were asked to produce a display of all the flags of the competing nations in World Cup 1986 staged in Mexico. As the teachers and other pupils knew that I was interested in flags, they asked me to bring in my books about flags so that they would have something to copy from. This was a case of one of my special interests being applied to a particular event in which most people were interested.

Football

By now, I had become interested in watching and playing football. Whereas I had previously been reluctant to take part in such activities, I now wanted to be part of things. Previously, I had never kicked a football, apart from when a ball happened to come my way in the yard or in the street where I lived. But I noticed that other pupils seemed to have no problem kicking a ball about between them and shouting names such as 'Lineker', 'Rush', 'Maradona' and others each time they scored. At first, I tried to make an effort to take part in a game, but each time I kept trying to kick a ball, I couldn't kick it in the direction that I intended. When playing football in PE lessons, having to dribble the ball around a set of cones was hard for me too. I had great difficulty in being able to keep control of the ball when going in between the cones often knocking the cones down. The other pupils often made fun of me when this happened. It wasn't long before they started to notice that I was gullible. They would say to me, 'Look Chris, there's a UFO,' and then throw the ball at my face.

Outside of school, my parents noticed that I was spending too much time in my room by myself and they were beginning to get concerned that I wasn't developing any social skills as well as not getting enough activity. They enrolled me and Alex, my brother, in a football coaching course. Alex very quickly mastered the basic skills and was quite a good player. When starting the coaching course, I found it very difficult to find a partner for activities that involved working in pairs, particularly as I didn't know anyone at first. Often, I worked together in pairs with Alex. Being a good player, Alex also interacted with other players around us much more easily, whereas I felt more left out. At first, in a game situation, I couldn't understand where my role was within the team. The other players wouldn't pass me the ball and when I did get the ball, I couldn't keep it under control and the opponents often picked up the loose ball and scored. I found myself being blamed for conceding goals not knowing it was my fault. I had great difficulty in trying to interpret the body language of other players and knowing which position to move into off the ball.

Playground game-show host

In the playground, I was often very anti-social. Around me, other pupils were playing different games in groups. I couldn't understand what their purpose was and, as there were no written rules about how to take part, I didn't know what to do:

> 'Christopher continues to do his best work when apart from the class and it is noticeable that he fails to associate with anyone in the playground, having formed no lasting relationships.' Extract from School Report 1988.

Meanwhile, I liked to play imaginative games on my own, often copying scenes from my favourite television programmes. As well as *Thomas the Tank Engine and Friends*, I also enjoyed *Blockbusters*, a popular early afternoon quiz show on UK television hosted by Bob Holness. Of many things that I liked to pretend to be sitting while on the edge of the playground, one of these was Bob Holness presenting *Blockbusters*. Occasionally, other pupils would notice me playing on my own on the edge of the playground and there were some that joined in. What I didn't realise at the time was that many of the other pupils were laughing at me rather than with me thinking that I was very strange, as my behaviour and traits were very unusual. However, there were two other pupils that appeared to enjoy playing *Blockbusters* with me, Dale and Andrew. Dale also had an interest in trains, and liked some of the questions. Like me, he was also a slow academic developer and he was also made fun of by other pupils but for different reasons, so he could relate to me better than most. Andrew, who was very strong academically, also liked reading for information and was very understanding of Dale and I.

Inter-cities

As well as *Blockbusters*, Dale and I often liked to play Inter-Cities in the playground, using the drains as the track. Dale, like me, had had a Christmas present of a Hornby Inter-City 125. Occasionally, my parents took me on weekend trips to London to visit relatives. I loved to travel on the Inter-City 125, as I liked the way that the carriages were arranged with their blue and cream liveries together with the British Rail (BR) double-headed arrow logo and the way that their interior was arranged in terms of the tables and seats. In the middle, there was the buffet car that had different shaped windows.

An aspect of BR Inter-City network (now privatised) that I also liked was the stations that it served and I liked the loudspeaker within the train that the guard used to announce which station the train was arriving at. I particularly liked to memorize all the announcements. And when playing Inter-Cities, Dale was the driver and I was the guard, where I got to make all the announcements. These were the only times when I interacted with others in the playground. I used to like to take up other roles that I had seen on trains and in railway stations, such as being one of the catering staff pushing the trolley saying, 'Coffee and sandwiches.'

When playing such games, we often found ourselves being mocked by other pupils, who preferred to play different and sometimes more daring games. Often, other pupils liked to 'hijack' the train by throwing litter at us and then knocking us 'off the rails'. When I was with either Dale or Andrew, I had the security of somebody being around me. However, when on my own (which was usually the case) and being intimidated by bullies, I would occasionally loose patience and over-react, which often ended up in a fight.

2

Moving House and School:
A Traumatic Change

This was the most difficult change that I have had to cope with to date. The last house change that my family had was difficult enough for me, but this time, I was old enough to experience the effects of change. My parents were starting to feel frustrated about living in Washington. Being a new town, Washington felt very isolated.

This time we were moving to Sunderland. Although I wasn't happy at school and had had great trouble making friends with other pupils my age, I felt that I had become settled in the home where we lived and felt secure, with my books and train set with which I could amuse myself, to compensate for very rarely having friends around to play. Like when being moved from Stockton to Washington when younger, moving house was again fearsome to me, as I would have to get used to a new school and a new living environment. So that I had an idea of what to expect when changing schools, a visit to my new school in Sunderland, Fulwell Junior School, was arranged. Here I met the head teacher, Miss F, and Mrs M, who was to be my class teacher.

Problem child

When in the process of moving house, my parents arranged for me and my brother and sister to stay with our aunt, uncle and cousins, who lived in New Hartley, Northumberland. When staying with our relatives, the Shandran family, I found myself left out when my brother went to play football with the three Shandran boys and their friends. A sports-orientated family, the three Shandran boys, like my brother, were all good footballers. In this sense, I felt left out because I couldn't be part of things. At home, this wouldn't normally be a problem as I had my books and my train set to amuse myself with. But at the Shandran's house, I didn't have any of this, as it was all packed into tea chests in a removal van. When I couldn't find anything to keep me occupied, I started to reject the place that didn't suit me by behaving childishly.

To the Shandrans, it must have seemed like a Problem Child movie, only that it was real, as were the effects. In once instance, I flooded the bathroom by leaving the taps running and in another, I woke everybody up in the middle of the night throwing water bombs out of the window onto the garage roof.

I didn't realise that the water wasn't good for the flat garage roof. Probably the worst thing that I did though was throwing some of my cousin's clothes out of the window into the garden. Looking back, I don't think that I did this intentionally or to spite anyone, but I just felt that it was a reaction to how I felt about moving house and not being able to amuse myself during the procedure.

Once the removal men had unloaded all of our contents into our new house and I was taken there with my brother and sister, my parents heard all about my behaviour at the Shandrans and were furious with me. When seeing how my parents felt about it, I began to realise what I had done. However, once all my belongings were unpacked and I was introduced to my new room, I calmed down as I had a place where I knew I could go to have solitude. I was so glad to be able to see all my books together with my trains. This partly helped me to get settled into my new environment.

Foreign dialect?

After a summer holiday, it was soon time for me to start at my new school. My parents saw this school transition as a chance for me to make a new start and they kept 'pressing' me to behave myself. Two of my new classmates gave me a brief introduction to the school, showing me where everything was. At first, I made an attempt to get to know the other pupils, but they noticed that I spoke very differently.

Something that I never developed, and never have developed despite living in Sunderland for most of my life, was a local dialect. My actual dialect is something that has puzzled many people who have known me. I tended to speak slower and clearer than others, and other pupils spoke in the Sunderland dialect (Mackem). Many of them started to ask me where I was originally from and one person even asked me which country was I from! Meanwhile, Alex had also started at Fulwell and he found it much easier to make friends as he had quickly picked up the Mackem accent, or at least sounded local enough to feel accepted. When people found out that Alex and I were brothers, they couldn't believe it, as not only were we not alike in terms of appearance, but Alex seemed to have adapted quickly to the local environment, whereas I might as well have joined the school directly from another planet rather than being moved just a few miles down the road.

Other pupils, on noticing how different I sounded, started taunting me by 'echoing me', making fun of something that I felt I had no control over. It was perfectly normal for me to speak this way, as this was the way that the words I was saying were written, whereas they weren't often written as they would perhaps be pronounced in a particular local dialect. As the echoing escalated, the more it began to irritate me and it eventually got to the point where I would over-react and start a fight. Sometimes I would even end up starting fights with pupils who were genuinely trying to be friendly with me. I only realised this after Mrs Mann reassured me.

Parental pressure

Back at home, my parents noticed that my brother and sister had very quickly made friends at their new school and often had friends around after school and at weekends. Much of my time outside of school was again spent alone in my room. My brother particularly liked playing games in groups of people, including football and cricket. My parents kept encouraging me to join in, not often realizing why I was reluctant to. I often preferred to play games that I could play on my own, in particular snooker. My parents often asked me if anybody at school liked playing snooker, but I didn't feel comfortable playing with someone my own age who might make fun of how hopeless a player I was. I often preferred to play with a grown-up who was often more likely to be more encouraging when playing shots.

My parents also began to think that the reason why I wasn't making any friends was because of the way I spoke. Constantly, they kept correcting me each time I said something that 'didn't sound right'. This only encouraged me to shut myself off even more from people around me, as it irritated me just as much as other pupils echoing me. This caused a huge problem, when having to do homework that involved reading aloud to my parents, as rather than encourage me, they would just keep telling me to 'speak properly', and they didn't want to know when I kept trying to say that I couldn't help it.

What was most frustrating was that they weren't like this with my brother and sister when they had to read aloud for their homework. These speaking interventions got to me so much that I eventually stopped reading aloud to my parents as I felt I couldn't make any progress, so I preferred to read to myself. After I stopped reading aloud to my parents, they then accused me of not doing my homework at all and not even bringing it home. They kept saying to me that the reason why they did this was to make me more like the other kids, but I was content with the way I was. I was being 'got at' by my own parents for something that other kids were making fun of me for!

Progress through small group sessions

Academically, I began to make progress in art and creative writing, but still struggled with maths. Mrs Mann recognised this and arranged for me to have extra maths lessons during lunch times. These extra lessons were done in a small group of just four pupils including myself. The other three pupils in the group all felt that they had similar difficulties and we could relate to one another quite well. I found this environment much easier to work in and make progress and I felt able to concentrate more. Also, it felt a much lesser intimidating environment in which to ask for help. Often, in a full classroom situation, I felt too timid to ask for help being around so many other pupils who I felt were much more advanced than I was.

Through my extra maths lessons, I managed to bring myself up to an acceptable standard for my age and I could now apply mathematical skills to the solution of problems. For the first time, I was able to achieve above average test results. In turn, this reinforced my progress in other subjects such as science. I am very grateful to Mrs Mann to this day.

It had taken me a while to settle into Fulwell Junior School, but once I felt settled, I started to make progress, even in subjects that I had previously struggled with:

> 'Christopher abhors change and finds it difficult to settle down in a new class. However, once he feels secure, he can make progress.' Extract from school report, 1988

Sadly, by the time I was settled in, it was almost the end of term and it was soon time for me to make one of my most significant transitions to date, my transfer to secondary education.

3

Stepping into the land of Giants:
My Transition To Secondary School

Making the transition to secondary school was one of the most daunting changes that I ever had to face. Before I started at Monkwearmouth Comprehensive School, the headmaster Mr Farnie had visited Fulwell Junior School to give a talk about starting secondary school. This initially made me feel more reassured, especially when I found what he said encouraging. Also, I had had an induction day at Monkwearmouth so I had an idea of what to expect when I started. However, actually starting secondary school as a pupil was very different.

As well as noting the size of many of the older, bigger pupils that would be around me in the schoolyard, what intimidated me most of all was the size of the place. It was almost five times bigger than Fulwell Junior School and there were so many different classrooms and many more teachers. I was particularly worried that I might get lost in my first week and even more worried about what would happen if I did get lost. Would I get into trouble with a teacher or would I find myself walking into other, much bigger pupils who would do nasty things to me?

My parents, who had seen how I had difficulty making friends in primary school, were particularly worried about this aspect of me when starting comprehensive school. So that I wouldn't be alone in the schoolyard during lunchtime, they encouraged me to try and find some lunchtime clubs and activities. But finding my way around the school at first was difficult enough; I didn't know where to go for lunchtime clubs or what they involved.

Timetable overload

One of the most difficult aspects of secondary school that I had to get used to was the more varied nature of the learning programme, having to change classrooms and teachers for each different subject. Back in primary school, I had the security of being based in one classroom with a class teacher whom I had got to know, occasionally having different teacher for different subjects. Also, I found myself having to know my timetable of which lesson I was supposed to be at and which classroom I was supposed to be in.

The timetable that I had was based around week one and week two, and it changed every two weeks.

In my first few weeks at Monkwearmouth, I suffered much confusion. The two week timetable system confused me greatly and it was often a case of me getting mixed up with whether or not it was week one or week two. In some cases, I found myself bringing the wrong books to the wrong lessons! This made me feel very stupid, and it wasn't helped when other pupils laughed at me. In some cases, other pupils would take advantage of this, especially when they noted my gullibility. They would tell me which lesson we would have next, which wasn't the actual lesson we were supposed to have next, and I found myself going to the wrong classes, which were sometimes classes for older pupils. It felt so embarrassing, especially when I found myself in a class of older pupils who told me to go back to the junior school where I belonged. So that I would be sure of having the right books at the right lessons, I started to take all my books with me to school every day. I found myself carrying a heavy load to school with me each day.

Lonesome imagination

Much of my time in the schoolyard at Monkwearmouth was spent on my own, like in primary school. However, whereas most other kids had grown out of imaginative play by the time they had started secondary school, it was still a way for me to amuse myself during break-times. At first, I found myself unable to interact with other pupils because I couldn't relate to their topics of conversation, which were usually about pop music and video games, two pastimes that I didn't know anything about.

While I was still watching children's programmes, my peers had moved onto watching the Australian soap operas *Neighbours* and *Home and Away*, and were also into action films such as *Robocop* and *Top Gun*. Like I had done in primary school, I often found myself sitting on the edge of the playground, often imitating what I had seen in my favourite television programmes. Programmes that I liked to imitate were those that I used to watch when I came home from school each afternoon. These programmes included children's programmes, such as *The Sooty Show*, *Mike n' Angelo*, *Knightmare* and many others. Another programme that I had spent the summer holidays watching that I liked to imitate was *Wacaday*. During the summer holidays, whereas my brother and sister had friends they could call on, I was usually left on my own in my room, reading or watching television.

While I was playing my imaginative games by myself, other kids around me had moved on to the more 'rough and tumble' style of play, often wrestling.

At first, second year girls noticed that I was pretending to be Timmy Mallett presenting *Wacaday*. Eventually, others noted that I was imitating *The Sooty Show* and it wasn't long before I had a huge crowd of people around me, which I didn't at first take notice of, as it was normal for me to play like this. What I was blind to was what they thought of me and when they were laughing, I didn't realise that they were mocking me. My play appeared rather childish compared to their preferred rougher, more aggressive play. Mr Farnie saw what was happening and broke up the crowd. It was only after he told me how I was coming across to other pupils that I realised they were just having a laugh at me thinking that I was weird.

Early frustrations in secondary school

In primary school, I had begun to like watching and playing football. However, I never had the confidence to go in for trials for the school football team, as by the time I had worked out how to play the game, the football season was over. This time though, I felt I had the confidence to go in for trials. Hopefully, if I could make an impression, it could gain me some more respect among the other pupils, who had previously taunted me for being clumsy. Unfortunately, I didn't make either the first or second team. Meanwhile, my brother, who was still in the junior school, had made it onto the first team and I can remember being very envious. My cousins all played for their school teams and one had also started playing Sunday league football. I felt particularly frustrated that they had games to look forward to playing in every weekend, while I didn't. Rarely would I go and watch my brother or cousins playing football, unless my parents forced me to come along. It just felt so frustrating to watch them getting to do something that I couldn't be part of.

Growing up in Sunderland, a football-orientated place, being able to play football is often paramount to fitting in at school. I was still very clumsy at playing the game and I often showed 'tunnel vision' when playing, in being only able to see the ball rather than the body-language of my team mates and opponents. Very rarely would a player pass me the ball and when I did get the ball, there was often only one thing on my mind, which was to run with it and try and score. I didn't know who to pass to as I had great difficulty being able to read the positional sense and movement of the ball. When running with the ball, I often found myself losing it and the opposition would often pick up the loose ball and go on to score.

As much as I had begun to like playing different sports, PE lessons were often very difficult for me. When picking teams, I often found myself being the last person to be picked and when doing activities that involved working in pairs, the teacher often had to find a partner for me.

Elsewhere, a subject that I had been particularly looking forward to was science. Having previously had a Christmas present of a chemistry set, I became fascinated by scientific equipment (for example, test tubes, Bunsen burners and so on) and was eager to use it. Science also related to my interest in astronomy. However, when starting science, I found that it was very different to the science that I enjoyed to pursue in my spare time. It was much more based around weights and measures and as I was very poor at maths, I began to struggle with it. When I found that I wasn't happy with weighing and measuring, I began to get sidetracked into other areas of the subject that I found very interesting, but unfortunately, weren't part of the syllabus. When the teacher intervened to try and get me to focus on the task in hand, I began to react childishly. This got me into a lot of trouble.

> 'At times he has produced very good work and has shown a commendable depth of knowledge and interest. However, his progress will be slow if he does not learn to concentrate on the task in hand. Recently, he has been childish and silly, almost to the point of being a disruptive influence on the class.' Extract from school report, 1990.

I felt it was a case of the rigid nature of the National Curriculum not being suited to the way that I liked to practice scientific experiments, as I liked to try many different ideas that weren't relevant. As a result, I began to lose interest in science and my progress in the subject became very slow.

Frustrations in social life

Back at home, my parents were becoming increasingly concerned about me spending too much time to myself in my room or watching television. They were especially worried that I didn't have much scope in which to develop social skills. My brother and sister, meanwhile, appeared to have many friends round or were often round at a friend's house. My cousins, each time we went around to seen them, also appeared to be with friends most of their time. In this sense, I was the 'odd one out' as I stayed put most of my time. The longer this went on, the more my parents even started to 'force' me to invite friends round for a game of snooker (we used to have a snooker table), often not realising why I wasn't prepared to. In one instance, they even forced me to ring a friend, not realising that I didn't particularly like using the telephone, and stood over me when I made the call. It was only made worse when they kept on at me to speak properly and use the appropriate telephone manner.

So that I would be around other pupils outside school hours, my parents suggested joining Monkwearmouth Youth Club. At first, I was slightly reluctant to go, as I would come across other kids who had been mean to me in the schoolyard, but when I found out about the activities that I could do, such as swimming, skiing and so on. I decided to give it a try.

In the schoolyard, because the pupils are under the control of teachers and school rules, having to wear a uniform, it is often a case of having to find a way to exert superiority over others in the pecking order. This can be ruthless and aggressive, especially when trying to prove themselves as the hardest or coolest kids in the school. I was particularly vulnerable to other pupils trying to exert such superiority over me. Joining Monkwearmouth Youth Club enabled me to see other kids my age away from the confines of school rules and school uniform.

Remarkable memory

As the other kids got to know me better, their attitudes towards me during school hours changed a little. Something that they and many of the teachers, in particular the PE teacher Mr Walter, found out about me that they liked was that I had a remarkable memory for sporting facts and figures. I could answer just about any football trivia question that I was presented with, knowing who won the FA Cup each year as well as all the World Cup records. I may have been clumsy at playing football and many other sports and envied those who were good at playing the game, but I had something that they envied, my memory. As well as winning me some prizes at football trivia competitions, it also gained me a lot of respect among pupils and teachers:

> 'In his defence, he has managed to gain considerable respect for his amazing sporting memory bank.' Extract from school report, 1990.

Former World Snooker Champion Steve Davis was also impressed with my memory for sporting facts and figures when he came to open the school fair. One of the teachers had told him that I was a 'mastermind of sport'. When I met him, he asked me when he first won the Snooker World Championship. He was not only impressed that I knew the year (1981), his opponent (Doug Mountjoy) and the score (18-12), but he also said that I knew more about his career than he did!

Mixed fortunes

Going to the youth club helped me become a little more confident at trying different activities at school. Another subject that I had grown to like was drama because I really liked acting out other roles and it was one of few areas in which I felt I could work well with others. Perhaps the role or character that I was playing masked who I really was. That year, the school was putting on a production of *The Wizard of Oz*. I knew the story well as I had enjoyed the film that starred Judy Garland. My favourite character was the Tin Man and I auditioned for the part, memorizing all the song lyrics. I was just beaten to it by a fifth year pupil, but the teachers were so impressed with my effort that they gave me an effective minor role, the Munchkin leader. I enjoyed being part of *The Wizard of Oz*. Since starting school, it was the first time where I felt that I was able to make a valuable contribution.

Elsewhere, Mr Walter, the PE teacher, saw that I was really making an effort to become more involved in activities with others. He invited me to go on a school trip with the other school football teams to watch Liverpool play at Anfield. For this trip, he asked me to organise a football quiz that the other kids could take part in. He was very impressed with the way I organised thes questions and the other kids enjoyed taking part. En route to Liverpool the team played a series of games against some teams from Wigan and I was given a few minutes as a substitute in one game. It was the only time that I ever got to play football in an organised team situation. When I came on with five minutes to go, the team were leading 2-1, but with my first involvement, I gave away a free-kick which led to a goal and then right at the end, I gave the ball away in my own half which led to us being beaten 3-2! I got a bit of stick from the other players afterwards as I had lost them the game, but despite this, I really liked the experience of being able to play in an actual match situation. For me, this was equivalent to a professional winning his only England cap. Watching Liverpool play Southampton at Anfield was a great experience. Liverpool won the game 3-2.

However, after the Anfield trip and the production of *The Wizard of Oz* were over, it was back to being in the schoolyard all on my own again. I didn't particularly like eating lunch with other pupils in case they taunted me or threw things at me, so I started coming home for lunch. I sometimes found myself being threatened by other pupils on my walk home, but at least once I got home, they couldn't get to me there and for half-an-hour, I had an escape from the harsh reality of the schoolyard. When being teased, I still had difficulty in being able to control my temper and would often start a fight. The more I started fights, I found myself being put on report and having to have it signed by my tutor and head of house before leaving for home each day. The report sheet was just a piece of paper, but to me it felt like a chain.

Starting all over again

After I had had my 'settling in' year at Monkwearmouth, it was now time for me to calm down. The summer holidays had again seen me spending a lot of time on my own, as I didn't have any friends whom I could contact. Accusing me of wasting my holiday, my parents kept on at me to try and take part in activities with other people my age and try to 'get in' with a group of friends, but I still didn't know how, as it wasn't clear as to how to fit in with a particular group of people.

When going back to school to start my second year, I noticed that I was no longer in the second year, but in Year 8. The incorporation of the National Curriculum had seen the first year become Year 7, and the second, third, fourth and fifth years had become Year 8, Year 9, Year 10 and Year 11 respectively. This was very confusing for me. When writing my name on exercise books and on registration forms, I had been used to writing my tutor group as 1RP, which was now 8RP. Starting Year 8, I initially forgot that I was no longer in 1RP and I was still putting my tutor group down as 1RP. In a French lesson, I even ended up signing the registration form twice, after my classmates had passed it back to me saying that I needed to sign it twice to 'make sure'. I was gullible enough to believe this. When the teacher noticed, he thought that I was being stupid, but I didn't intend it. This gave my classmates another opportunity to laugh at me.

By now, I was gradually learning how to control my temper and not to over-react when provoked. This time, I wanted to concentrate a little more on my work. Teachers experienced much confusion with me as some saw me as above average in arts and humanities subjects such as English and history while others saw me as rather backward in the more technical subjects such as science and maths. My parents had organized for me to have a personal tutor for maths, from whom I benefited greatly, but the subject that I was struggling with was science.

When starting at Monkwearmouth, science had been the subject that appealed to me the most, but now I had lost interest in it so much that I was having great difficulty with some of its concepts. One of the reasons why I felt I struggled with scientific concepts was largely through my tunnel-vision. Interpreting scientific formulae when working out compounds, for example, I felt that I just needed to follow the formula as it was on a formula sheet, but on the formula sheet, I couldn't see the actual workings of the formula, which are invisible. I found that if I asked for help when stuck, I started to understand the subject better and after a struggle, I eventually brought myself up to a standard that was acceptable for Year 8.

Frustrations in family life

Back at home, my parents were still pushing me to get myself out more, especially when my brother and sister were often out with friends. They tried enrolling me in all different kinds of activities, some of which I was prepared to try out, but some which I had no interest in at all. At first, I took part in five-a-side football at the local leisure centre, where my brother also took part. When playing five-a-side football, I liked playing the game, but I felt very inferior being around a group of good players. What was perhaps worse for me was that I had a younger brother who was a really good player. Not being able to match his ability used to frustrate me so much, especially when he won many trophies and medals and I didn't have anything. This made me have some terrible tantrums.

A form of football that I could play on my own was Subbuteo. I liked to create my own fantasy World Cup competitions in my own stadium, away from taunting of others and having to put up with being envious of having good players around me. As well as being able to memorise the commentary so well, I liked to collect the different Subbuteo team colours. Like model railways created an imaginary world for me to retire to when I couldn't be understood in the real world, Subbuteo provided me with my own football arena, when others wouldn't let me join in their games.

I was also enrolled in a table tennis coaching programme with my brother and sister, who mastered the basic skills very quickly while I was left behind. Again, my brother showed great ability in the game and continued to win many medals and trophies and his trophy shelf in his bedroom was getting larger, while I had no trophies and medals to display. This frustrated me throughout my upbringing. I was physically the oldest of three, but mentally, I felt like I was the youngest.

New subject interests

At school, I was starting to enjoy some lessons, in particular history and geography. I enjoyed history because I liked researching the past and my teacher, Mr Coulson, often used to use some effective idioms to illustrate what he was teaching. For instance, when talking about Anno Domini (AD) and the origination of the Georgian dating system, he used the idiom 18YASWTFAC, which meant the year 1991 represented 18 years after Sunderland won the FA Cup in 1973! I was becoming much more enthusiastic about my schoolwork, particularly with subjects that I liked. However, my efforts often didn't get me the results and grades I probably deserved:

'... he has good general knowledge and it is specific things that let him down. Consequently, I was a little disappointed with the exam. He deserved a better grade.' Extract from school report, 1991.

Gradually, I was settling down at school and I was starting to make some new friends. When I had a few friends around me, I found that I wasn't an easy target for bullying and I managed to pick up some social skills that were acceptable to other kids. For a while, I did have some friends who came round for a game of snooker. This kept my parents off my back for a while about not having any friends, but little did I know that things were about to change in terms of growing up.

4

Changing Body Shapes:
Adolescence

When I started Year 9, I noticed that other pupils around me where slowly starting to change. My peers appeared to be developing new and different interests and were also developing different instincts. Habits and topics of conversation were also changing and I was finding myself not being able to keep up with it all. While my peers were becoming interested in things that many people appear to develop an interest in during adolescence, such as fashion and the opposite sex, I was still watching *Thomas the Tank Engine and Friends, Wacaday* and *The Sooty Show*. While my peers were taking their first steps towards becoming adults, such as placing more emphasis on fashion, appearance and style, at around the age of 14, I still felt like a little kid, as I didn't know what doing such things with hair and dress sense was about.

Often, I think that my peers saw having anything to do with me as taking a 'step back', as I still behaved like a Year 7 pupil at times in terms of how unsure I was of myself and looked very young for my age. Whereas much of the bullying I had faced when starting secondary school was about other kids having to assert their authority within the pecking order, bullying in adolescence was different. It was more about other kids asserting who was the most 'grown up' within the pecking order.

Insular social interaction

The only times that I saw other kids my age was during school hours. Very rarely did I see other people that I went to school with outside school, so I didn't know what was considered fashionable or 'naff' to wear. This often caused problems when going shopping with my mother for new clothes. My mother, who was very interested in clothes and fashion, liked people dressing up smartly. She kept asking me what other kids wore for smart dress code for formal family events. I didn't know as I never saw anybody else my age in such situations and I couldn't understand why I needed to dress smartly away from school, as I felt that I wasn't old enough for this sort of thing. This often frustrated my mother greatly and she would end up taking the easy way out by blaming me for not having any friends and saying that it was an embarrassment to be seen with someone dressed the way I was. What I particularly hated was when she kept correcting my dress sense in public, making me tuck my shirt in properly and wear my jacket properly rather than loosely. She was rarely like this with my brother and sister.

By now, my brother had started at Monkwearmouth and he appeared to have no problems making friends. He made more new friends in just a few months than I had in nearly three years. As he had a group of friends around him, he wasn't a target for bullying and could settle in to the comprehensive school environment much quicker than I had been able to.

Not seeing my peers much outside of school hours also meant that I couldn't relate to their topics of conversation and the interests they had developed. I didn't know what they were like outside school hours or what they did. Most of my time outside school hours was spent alone, often in my room reading. Back at school, I was again becoming a target for bullying, as I was immature for my age. Other kids, including kids who had previously been bullied or would have otherwise been bullied in my absence, found it fun to threaten and intimidate me. I wasn't too keen to go out outside school hours in case somebody from school saw me and threatened me.

Threats and intimidation one

At school I was facing much teasing and intimidation from other pupils, which led me to doing something that I still regret to date. During science, a group of pupils were intimidating me with all sorts of threats and as they started pushing me, I reacted and ended up stabbing another pupil in the eye with a pen. This action saw me excluded and I knew that my life was never going to be the same again, in the sense that I would be vilified for the rest of my school life by my peers. I could very easily have blinded the pupil that I stabbed. Feeling more isolated than ever, I feared that I would be taken away to a special school. This was the most difficult time of my life to date. I felt that I had nobody to whom I could go to for help, except perhaps my mother, who had seen how difficult it was for me to get on and make friends with other people my age and knew that I wasn't intentionally a trouble maker. As a special needs teacher, she made an effort to understand what I was going through during this time.

To my surprise, I managed to gain re-admittance to school quite quickly. Mr Farnie had heard about the incident from the deputy head and arranged for me to come back to school with my mum where he could ask me some questions. At first, I felt frightened about coming back to school, where many people would have been happy to see the back of me, but I was surprised at how well Mr Farnie handled it. He talked to me, rather than at me. This made me feel much better and I felt able to come back to school. However, I soon found myself a target for much vilification. Many other pupils kept telling me that I should have been expelled and that other schools would have had me thrown out ages ago. For a while, Mr Farnie allowed me to spend my break-times indoors where I would be away from the taunting of others.

Literal learning

During Year 8, I felt that I had made progress in some areas, especially in my stronger subjects, but in Year 9, I was finding some of the work a little harder. This often occurred when having to interpret material under study with imagination rather than just explaining, in other words reading between the lines. For instance, when analyzing texts or historical sources, I was able to see what was actually written or displayed, but couldn't often understand their hidden meaning or what they were trying to convey. Often, I would become very confused if there wasn't a right or wrong answer.

During lessons, I often worked to the best of my ability. Sometimes, my tendency to interpret instructions literally was a problem, especially during assessment tests:

> 'Christopher works very hard, and also very meticulously, to the extent that he can mistake instructions by reading them very literally – had he not done this in his exam, he would have had a 'B' grade.' Extract from school report, 1992.

Heavy metal

When starting comprehensive school, I found that I had a 'way in' with other pupils with my memory for football trivia, which I still had. By now though, I had developed another interest that was acceptable to other kids my age – rock/heavy metal music. I had grown to like the angry and aggressive sound of this type of music, which at first provided an anecdote to the classical music that had been 'enforced' on me by my parents and in music lessons at school. I liked being a 'headbanger'. When some other pupils noticed by chance that I liked bands such as Iron Maiden, Guns N' Roses, Nirvana and others their attitude towards me changed.

This interest wasn't acceptable to my parents at times though. At one point, I wanted to have my ear pierced, but they wouldn't let me. Personally, I found this rather hypocritical, especially when they kept trying to make me more acceptable to other kids by telling me to 'speak properly'. But when I said that I would be more like the other kids if I did have my ear pierced, they didn't want to know. At least when I dressed up in the appropriate dress code of a bandana, studs and a patched denim jacket, I looked as though I belonged to a teenage cult.

Inadequacies in language and sexuality

It wasn't long though before the headbanger (or 'mosher', as it was known) gang found out about my inadequacies. Wearing a similar dress code to other moshers, I appeared to be one of the gang, but socially, I couldn't understand their 'lingo'. As much of what I spoke was of written origination, I didn't pick up swear words, so I didn't understand the meaning of them. Eventually, I began to pick up bad language once I knew what it meant. But what I still hadn't understood though was being able to know where and when not to use such language. In some cases, I even spoke such language to my parents.

The next inadequacy that the mosher gang noticed was that I often didn't know how to use such bad language independently, the way they did, and that what I was often doing was just repeating what I had heard. When they found this out, they immediately saw me as a target for wind-ups, often playing dirty tricks on me that got me into trouble. They encouraged me to do things that I didn't often realise were rude and even illegal, such as exposing myself. Often, their games included 'truth or dare', which was a way for them to express sexuality and their interest in the opposite sex. They talked about the opposite sex, something they were developing an interest in. I had never really noticed the opposite sex in this way and they began to think that I was very strange when I didn't show any such interest. They showed me pictures of women that they had cut out of magazines and asked me which ones I found attractive. I felt embarrassed to say anything in this situation, and it wasn't long before they started asking me if there were any girls at school I liked. When I said that I hadn't noticed the girls at school, they started 'pairing me up' with girls, another way in which they wound me up.

Threats and intimidation two

Eventually, when they noticed that I didn't appear to get turned on by girls, they started to think that I was perhaps gay. But it wasn't as if I was attracted to boys. There are many places where it perhaps isn't considered acceptable to be a homosexual and of places where it is most unacceptable, the schoolyard is one. Once the suggestion that I might be gay became common knowledge throughout the school, I became an immediate target for persecution, especially from the kids who considered themselves to be the hardest.

30

Due to the rumours about me I found myself facing much intimidation. I couldn't go anywhere within the school premises without being pushed or shoved. Even outside of school, when doing my paper round, I found myself being confronted by people who knew me at school. Yet it wasn't as if I meant any threat to them or anyone else. Often, I found that I didn't have an effective verbal or physical defence in these situations. Due to the sensitive nature of the issue, I felt too embarrassed to tell a teacher about what I was facing.

Eventually, a group of pupils hunted me down in the schoolyard. At first they wound me up, getting me to 'admit' that I was gay by forcing me to say that I was. When I said that I was, I only did so that they wouldn't physically harm me, yet they threw punches at me and I couldn't hit back. It was bad for their tribe if they didn't beat up 'the queer' and it took Mr Farnie to sort it out. Thankfully I only had a little more than a year of school left and it wasn't long before I would be sitting my GCSEs.

5

Coming Out of Childhood:
Final Year of Secondary School and into Further Education

After going through a very difficult period of my life between the ages of 13 to 14, I felt that I needed to make a fresh start elsewhere, where nobody knew about my reputation or my past. However, my father didn't want me to move schools as he didn't want me to leave Monkwearmouth with the reputation that I had picked up, thinking that it wouldn't be good for me or for the school.

Looking back, I think that changing schools would have probably been very difficult for me, as I would have had to get used to a new environment within a very short time. As I was in the process of studying my GCSEs, it would have also disrupted my studies. Since I only had another year left before I would be out of secondary school for good, there wasn't really much point. It was clear that I wasn't going to leave school with any friends.

Academically, I was becoming very conscientious in my work towards my final exams, as I really wanted to get good grades. When I could, I went to lunchtime classes where I was able to receive more individual attention. I felt less pressurised when there wasn't a class of others around me, enabling me to concentrate more. During classes, I tended to sit at the front so that I could concentrate on what the teacher was trying to convey, and also so that if anybody tried to provoke me, the teacher would be in a good position to see it and do something about it. By now, I had realised that if I behaved myself and worked hard, the teachers would appreciate me more and that school rules were in place for this reason. I started to get on so much better with the teachers than my peers, particularly when they saw how eager I was to work hard. However, as hard as I worked, I often became, if anything, too over-enthusiastic in my studies:

> 'Chris has a lively imagination and he is perceptive, although his response is sometimes idiosyncratic.' Extract from school report, 1993.

Academic misinterpretations

Often, I didn't see the purpose of specific tasks and exams. When I first took mock exams, I felt that the purpose of the exam was for the person taking the exam to express his or her knowledge on the subject concerned, rather than to measure ability. Having done so much revision for exams, I wanted to show how much work I had done by expressing it. Not realising it at the time, I found myself repeating what I had revised rather than applying it to the question:

> 'Christopher has shown great interest and effort over the year with outstanding term work. It is difficult to understand why he didn't do even better in the examination.' Extract from school report, 1993.

Elsewhere, when taking my English mock exam, one of the questions asked me to review a book that I had recently read. Not realising that this was meant to be a book I had studied in my English lessons, which happened to be William Golding's *The Lord of the Flies*, I wrote a review of a book connected with one of my interests, which was former England cricket captain Graham Gooch's autobiography. Although my teacher said it was a good review, I didn't realise that in this situation I could have asked one of the invigilators if I wasn't sure of the context of such a question.

I was unaware that there were particular skills and techniques required to pass an exam, such as managing the time allocated in which to complete the exam and to use the number of marks offered for each question as a guide to how much detail one needed to provide in the answer. I found that if I practiced taking past exam papers under examination conditions when studying, I managed to pick up some of these techniques.

Easy target

I was becoming more socially isolated during my final year at secondary school and, often, I didn't realise it. I was unable to relate to topics of conversation and only saw my peers during school hours. Outside of school, I was still very frightened to go out, even if it meant walking up the street, in case I came across someone from school that might try to get at me. Apart from going to watch football matches at Sunderland AFC, the only times I went out were to go to school. Meanwhile, my peers appeared to be advancing socially, talking about going out to the beach in large groups, going to rock/pop concerts, clothes shopping, going out on dates and so on.

The more other kids saw me on my own, the easier a target I was becoming for bullying. Often, on my way home from school, walking through a cemetery, a group of big kids would hide behind trees and jump on me. Most afternoons after coming out of school, I found myself having to alter my route home to avoid the bullies. However, they still followed me wherever I went. Maybe they had nothing better to do than to attack someone who liked his own company and meant no threat to anyone. I didn't realise that other kids at school didn't like those who didn't mix in, seeing them as strange or odd.

My self-esteem had been greatly harmed from bullying, but I was prepared to persevere with my studies. I wanted to get good results so badly but after each exam, I came out very low on confidence, feeling that I hadn't done particularly well. After I finished my last exam, I thanked all my teachers for all their help and for giving up their lunchtimes to give extra lessons, as they were very patient with me. There were times while at Monkwearmouth when I would have felt relieved to finally leave after what I was going through. It was only then how much I realised I would miss my teachers, including the headmaster Mr Farnie, as he had coped well with me through some of my most difficult times and offered plenty of encouragement in my studies.

Isolation and lack of self-direction

Now that I had left school, I could finally get away from having to be around certain people whom I felt had made my life a misery for almost five years. Now I could start to pursue my own interests. A sport that I was beginning to develop a strong interest in was cricket. During my summer holidays, I often found myself watching it on television. I became addicted to it and all its jargon and facts and figures. I particularly liked the way that the scorecards were structured and displayed on the screen, with the batting order down the left side and their scores down the right side. In between was how they lost their wickets. With my memory, I found I could also memorise test match scorecards well.

Previously, I had been to cricket matches when my father had obtained tickets to Durham County Cricket Club through work, but I really wanted to take in the experience of being at a cricket match on my own. I started going to watch Durham CCC play, even if it meant having to get as many as three buses! I really enjoyed going to cricket matches as I liked the quiet and laid back atmosphere. I also liked filling in the scorecards and built up a passion for collecting players' autographs. Often, after matches, I asked cricketers to sign their pen-portrait in a Cricketer's Who's Who that I had. Soon, I had quite an extensive collection, which included Ian Botham, Graham Gooch, Courtney

Walsh, Allan Donald and many others. Watching cricket was providing me with an escape from the rough environment of the schoolyard I had just left.

My parents were pleased that I had found something to do that I enjoyed, but were still concerned about me not being involved very much – if at all – with other people my age. Often, I found that I preferred the company of older, wiser, people whom I saw at cricket matches. My parents were also concerned about what I was going to do now that I had left school. Initially, I had wanted to do 'A' levels, but I didn't feel confident enough that I would get good enough grades to be able to take 'A' levels, so my parents suggested foundation GNVQ courses. Subjects that were suggested included catering, which I dismissed immediately as being a chef didn't appeal to me at all. Sport and leisure was also an idea; I was interested in this but was put off when I found out that applicants had to be good at actually playing sport. Media studies was another suggestion, which related to my school work experience at the local newspaper, the *Sunderland Echo*.

Post school pressure

During my mid-teens, I had briefly developed a career ambition related to my interests, which was to be a sports reporter or perhaps even commentator on *Test Match Special* or *Match of the Day*. I felt that this was a field in which my knowledge and interest would be useful – I could be John Motson and Jonathan Agnew rolled into one! In their mid-teens, many people feel optimistic with their whole life ahead of them and I was no different in this sense. What I didn't realise back then was that, often, the optimism of the future fades into the reality of the present when you get a little older. Out of my (I thought) limited choices in Further Education, media studies seemed the most appropriate due to my ambition to become a sports reporter. Really though, I wanted to pursue 'A' levels in subjects that I really enjoyed such as geography and history but as I had struggled with exams at GCSE level, I didn't feel confident enough to take any at a higher level.

Whereas it is often the norm for most 16 year old school leavers to look for part-time, or in some cases full-time, work once leaving school, I didn't feel mature enough to be employed. My parents thought that my social skills needed improving and that I needed to learn responsibility and they forced me to look for jobs in shops and supermarkets. As well as not feeling mature enough to do a job, I also felt that if I did have a job in a shop or supermarket, I might end up having to serve people that knew me from school, which I didn't want. My parents, particularly my mother, were so forceful in trying to get me to look for a job that they stood over me when writing letters of application and it even got to the point where she asked for application forms every time she went into supermarkets before forcing me to fill them in. Also, my sister started to get on my back saying, 'You should have a job by now,' especially as my brother was working as a bell boy at the local hotel and one of my cousins was working in a supermarket and that she would be getting a job if she were my age. None of this did my self-esteem any good. If anything it only discouraged me from looking for work. Looking back, I don't think that I could have handled part-time employment when 16 years old, especially after what I had been through at school.

Pleasant surprise

It wasn't long now to go until I received my GCSE results. This was something that I had worried about during the entire summer. I was so sure that I wasn't going to get good results, I didn't feel confident enough to go up to the school to collect them. Instead, I preferred to have them posted to me. I didn't want to go up to school and find that I had failed while other kids who had made my school life a misery finding out that they had done well. The day I was supposed to go up to get my results from school, I went on a day out to Holy Island, off the coast of Northumberland, with my aunt, uncle and cousins to try and take my mind off potential disappointment. Instead, my mother went up to the school to request them on my behalf.

What I didn't realise when coming back from Holy Island was that a surprise celebration had been planned. My parents had an envelope waiting for me. My mother told me that Mr Farnie said that my results were excellent and that I really should open the envelope and see for myself. Hearing this, I felt confident to open up my results and I was delighted! I had passed seven of my nine GCSEs at grade 'C' and above! The most I felt that I could have hoped for a few months back was three or perhaps four. Rightfully, I felt proud of my achievement, as I felt that I had deserved it, not only for all the work I had put in, but for all I had been through. I never found out how my peers had done and I didn't particularly want to know. This was particularly difficult for my mother when she was asked by relatives and friends about how others had done and she often had to explain about how I didn't associate with my peers.

My GCSE results meant that I could now pursue an advanced GNVQ course at Monkwearmouth College of Further Education. Starting college meant that I could settle down with a new group of friends who didn't know about my past. When I enrolled for GNVQ Media Studies, the course leader had heard about my exam results and initially had me down for the intermediate level, noticing that I perhaps had a tendency to underestimate my ability. He also said that there were often some very individually-minded people with whom I may get on with and that the atmosphere would be much more accepting than what I had been used to at school.

New peer group

At first though, it was very difficult to make new friends. Most other students whom I studied with tended to keep themselves to themselves and had very different interests to me. Like when I was at school, my parents noticed that I wasn't talking about any new people that I had perhaps met and that I didn't appear to be interested in getting to know my course-mates. My sister, who had now started comprehensive school and had made a lot of new friends very quickly as well as being academically gifted, also noticed this and started to call me a 'hermit' who had no mates. Often, she would go on at me about how I wasn't anything like our cousin Andrew who has just turned 18 and had a wide circle of friends who attended his 18th birthday party. My brother, meanwhile, had his set of friends with whom he played football. Apart from college, I didn't have any activity to keep me occupied. This wasn't doing my self-esteem any good.

To try and increase my interaction with other pupils my age, my father, after finding a leaflet about recreational activities available at the college, suggested I take part. Rather patronisingly, he reeled off each recreational activity, none of which I was very interested in, especially since most of the activities that were on offer I had previously tried and didn't like. However, a much better opportunity for me to get to know my course-mates and other students came along in the form of a college field trip to London.

During the field trip, I felt that I got to know my tutors and my course-mates better, learning a little more about their interests as they learned a little more about mine. My tutors got to know me better as an individual and I also got to know some of the older students, one of whom was particularly interested in my specialist interest in sport and my aspirations to become a sports reporter. One of his housemates was in the process of starting *Universal Post*, a student newspaper in Sunderland, and was looking for a student sports reporter to cover sport at university and regional level. This sounded like fun, especially as I would get to meet some new people who were at university. I contributed to *Universal Post*, covering sports stories ranging from university sports competitions to Sunderland AFC. I ended up winning awards for my sports writing, as it was something I enjoyed. I also gained an idea of what university life might be like and started a portfolio. The thought of going to university had started to appeal to me.

6

Emerging Expectations:
Applying to University

Although my experience with *Universal Post* had been beneficial in many ways, there was something else that it was creating that I didn't realise at the time. After winning awards with *Universal Post*, I found that there was a new set of expectations surrounding me. When my tutors, peers and relatives talked about me, they suggested that I might become the next John Motson or that they would one day be buying newspapers to read my reports. As this was an ambition that I had, I at first took in such suggestions, but inside, I wasn't really sure what I wanted to do.

At college, I was developing a reputation for being a hard-working student. I was very enthusiastic in my approach to my studies and was consistently handing my assignments in on time to a high quality. Courtesy of the attitude that I was showing towards my studies and the progress I was making, I was told that I would be a strong candidate for university.

Limitation of choice

However, as the course I was doing was vocational, I felt very limited as to what I could apply for. Looking back, I felt that I could have perhaps done with better guidance about applying to university in relation to careers. At first, I applied to university courses on the basis of their content rather than how applicable they were to future careers. I felt that I wanted to pursue a more general degree in the sense that I felt I would learn more, but not having done varied 'A' levels, I probably wouldn't have been able to handle some of the content. As I had studied Media Studies, I felt that I was restricted to stick to the subject and pursue it at degree level.

At first, I applied to Media Studies degree courses at universities in Sheffield, Leicester and Birmingham. My tutors, meanwhile, said that in relation to the portfolio that I had built up with my work with the *Universal Post*, I should probably consider applying to Journalism courses and suggested a course at Darlington College of Technology, franchised by the University of Teesside. This particular course also included the National Council for the Training of Journalists (NCTJ) pre-entry certificate as well as a degree, so it would provide me with two qualifications and was supposed to be 'employer friendly'.

When applying to university, what I really wanted was the higher education experience of meeting other people from different backgrounds in a different place, as I had had real problems being able to make friends locally. The career issue wasn't my first priority. I was encouraged by my tutors and parents to become a journalist, to fulfill the potential that they thought I had and had got me thinking I had. They wanted me to go to Darlington School of Journalism, a place with an international reputation for journalist training. As much as I had enjoyed journalism at amateur level through *Universal Post*, I still wasn't entirely sure about whether I really wanted to do it as a career. Back then, I didn't feel as though I was sceptical enough to be able to consider the pros and cons of journalism and other careers.

Social outsider

The status that I was developing as a 'good student' was making me appear like an outsider at times to other students. While they went to the college refectory or to the pub, I preferred to go to the library and do research for my assignments. When I did join in with others at the refectory, I often found that I couldn't relate to their topics of conversation, which were mainly about films and music, two topics that I didn't really follow that much, as I was very focused on following sport, particularly cricket, something which my colleagues weren't really interested in.

During this phase, other people around me aged between 16 to 19 were starting to discover new pastimes such as nightclubbing, something that didn't really appeal to me, and were also taking to drinking, something which I wasn't too keen on. Additionally, they were also becoming interested in relationships and losing their virginity. I couldn't, and still often don't, understand how such relationships form. Being around such conversations was making me feel immature, in the social sense, even though academically I was often achieving higher grades.

To try and find out what other people with whom I went to college did, I sampled nightclubbing when a colleague invited me to his 18th birthday party, for which he had hired a nightclub in Sunderland. One of the requirements for this event was smart dress code otherwise I wouldn't have been allowed past the door by the bouncers. What I couldn't understand was why people went through the awkwardness of it all when they would probably end up getting drunk and being sick. Also, what I didn't know about nightclubbing was that you would normally get home by taxi, as by the time the club closed there were no buses or trains. I didn't know how to call a taxi, so I ended up walking all the way home. I was alert enough to make it home safely, but my parents became very concerned. I was more concerned for myself though, as something much worse could have happened. This put me off going out for a while.

Professional or academic?

Academically, I was continuing to obtain distinctions and I was also receiving offers from some of the universities that I had applied to. However, I was beginning to have some personal reservations about actually going away to university. I had become very used to the largely safe and domesticated environment in which I lived at home and started to feel concerned about having to adapt to potential change. But I still wanted to perhaps experience living in a different place and meeting other people from different backgrounds. There was one part of me that wanted to remain in the safe environment of home, and another that wanted to broaden my horizons and leave behind the ghosts of some of the unpleasantness that I felt my school life and upbringing at times had had. This saw me experience much personal turmoil.

Deciding which university I should go to was also a source of anxiety for me. I had received six offers for different places, but I wasn't sure which place to go to. One of the offers I had was an unconditional offer to study Journalism at Darlington. My tutors told me that they had given me this offer due to my experience, whereas they would have asked most other people for much higher grades, due to the high competition for places. What I didn't realise at the time was that Darlington was desperate to attract students' funding.

I was told many things about why Darlington College of Technology was supposed to be the most prestigious journalist training college in the country. But at the age I was (17, nearly 18), I found that I could not see through the hype and that all I could do was 'sit back' and believe it. Due to my tendency to repeat things that I had heard other people say, I often found myself repeating what I had been told about the college. Other advice that I was given was that this kind of course, a vocational subject, that offered two qualifications would almost certainly lead me into a job. Again, I swallowed this rather than attempting to be sceptical about it. My future was being played with but I didn't realise it at the time.

People's expectations of me were becoming unrealistically high, especially as I had won an award for Media Student of the Year. I had been falsely encouraged to believe that I had a bright future ahead of me as a journalist. Back then, there were things I now feel really should have been taken into consideration about this. For instance, my social skills were still largely under-developed. Also, I perhaps didn't have some of the personal qualities to be able to handle the 'rougher' side of journalism, such as ruthlessness and being able to be manipulative, two things which I have never considered myself being capable of.

7

Starting University:
An Early Misfit

There was great expectation in my skills now and Darlington was being pushed as the best option. Being based at Darlington also meant that I would be close enough to visit Sunderland to come home some weekends if I felt lonely. From the prospectus, I also got the idea that, being based at a franchise college, I would be in classes of just a few people, rather than being in lecture halls full of over a hundred students. In this environment, I felt that I would be able to concentrate more. Back then though, I didn't realise the cons of franchising in higher education, in particular that the facilities (for example, library, technology) at the franchise colleges were often inadequate for higher education courses.

One of my first tasks when starting university was finding suitable accommodation. My parents helped me with house-hunting in Darlington. After looking at different places, we decided on a place on the outskirts of Darlington above a chip shop, where catering and laundry services were provided. I felt that having such assistance during my first year would be beneficial while settling in.

Early problems

There was another student who rented a room in the property called Michael, from South Wales. This provided me with an opportunity to get to know someone my age from a different part of the country. Also, Michael was in the same position as me – not knowing anyone else around him in a new place – so it was helpful to have somebody to go to the enrolment with. Michael seemed very outgoing and eager to meet our course-mates for the next three years and I felt that he could provide me with a 'way in'. Once people had got to know him, they would get to know who he was living with during the term.

At first, I felt very nervous being in a different place and being around different people who were from different parts of the country. But I realised that it would take some getting used to for most of us, particularly those away from home for the first time. During my first two weeks, my settling in period was interrupted by events beyond my control. At the property where I was living, there was a domestic dispute between the landlord and landlady, after which the property was put up for sale. I had to find a new place to live after I had only been there for two weeks!

Through the college's accommodations service, I managed to find somewhere very quickly. Again, it was in the form of a rented room, which also included catering and laundry, but this time, there was just myself with the landlady. Not living with another student, I found it more difficult to interact with others and I also didn't have anybody to keep me 'informed' as to what was happening.

Early confusions

During my first few weeks at university, I was finding that it was largely a case of people being away from home and parental control for the first time who were enjoying the freedom. They too seemed to be interested in drinking and going to nightclubs. Whereas many teenagers might go through a period where they gradually become used to drinking and socialising, so that it becomes a key element of their life in later years, I had never been able to understand this. I again found myself not being able to relate to topics of conversation. Durham County Cricket Club was about the only thing that I felt able to talk about with any authority. Again, people started to think that I was a 'bore' when Durham's season finishing bottom of the table was all I talked about at times. I did find a conversational 'way in' though through football. I quickly found that most of my course-mates were football fans that supported their respective local teams from Arsenal to Stockport County. When they noticed that I was also a football fan and was good with football trivia, I found that I was able to have reciprocal conversations.

When starting journalism workshops, while my colleagues seemed to be able to master the basic skills of news writing very quickly, I found myself falling behind. I had great difficulty in being able to construct a newspaper report appropriately, as I couldn't tell the whole story in a short, to-the-point paragraph before explaining more. I had been used to writing in much longer sentences and had great difficulty in being able to keep my copy short. I found it very difficult to decide what detail to include and what detail to leave out when writing a news story. Often, when writing, I tend to go for detail rather than plot and structure, as I am able to see and remember detail much better. The other students were probably able to manage with mastering news writing because they had been used to telling their friends about something that had happened in a pub.

Out of place

A skill that I had to learn and what the tutors put so much emphasis on was shorthand. One of the reasons why I had been 'pushed' to study journalism by my parents was because it included shorthand, something that would be useful on my C.V. Having struggled with handwriting when at school, I had great difficulty in being able to adjust to the technique of being able to write shorthand, having to keep characters small. I often found it so much easier to take down notes the conventional way rather than having to make so much effort to produce shorthand. Very quickly, I found that I was 20 words-per-minute behind the class.

I was also finding the practical journalism workshops very difficult, not so much because I had difficulty writing, but I found that journalism was a very restrictive art and that I had to make copy readable for an audience, rather than it being of my own style and expression.

Very quickly, I was beginning to feel out of place at journalism school, not just in terms of being a slow developer, but also in terms of how under-developed my social skills were. I was finding it very difficult to make friends, especially as I didn't know very much about their likely interests, such as soap operas and music. Also, other students were finding part-time jobs (often in pubs/bars), something that I still didn't know how to obtain. In the case of working behind the bar, I perhaps didn't have the social skills or awareness to obtain a bar job. I tried to take part in activities that they enjoyed. I didn't like the taste of beer or lager, but I liked the sweeter taste of cider.

I ended up vomiting, which got me into trouble with my landlady. After this experience, whenever I went out (which was very rare), I just drank coke, which made me feel even more of an outsider.

New academic interests

Academically, I managed to find some subjects that I quite liked and became encouraged to pursue more. As well as having to take journalism modules, to obtain a degree I also had to take some more academic subjects. One of these was politics, something that introduced me to ideals that appealed to me, one of which was Marxism. I liked some of the ideals expressed in Marxism, in particular the ideal of 'each according to his ability, each according to his need.' My interest in finding out more about Marxism later introduced me to *Living Marxism* magazine (later known as 'LM'), the magazine of the Revolutionary Communist Party. Two ideals that the magazine promoted were freedom of speech and freedom of expression, two privileges that I never really felt that I had in my past. From finding out more about these and other civil liberties, I found out more about the importance of being able to stand up for myself.

Other academic subjects that I was starting to enjoy were criminology and modern history. Through my modern history classes, I became interested in Russian history, something that I initially knew very little about. Until then I had never really been introduced to it. I found myself reading around these subjects and absorbing many details in the process. Whereas I was struggling to master news writing, I found writing academic essays much easier as I could add more detail. I found news writing very restrictive in that a news article had to be short and to the point. But writing essays, I found that there was much more scope to add detail that I found very interesting and that I felt supported the argument that I was trying to put across.

Early quitting reservations

By Christmas, I was beginning to have reservations about my course. I wondered if I would be better off doing something that was more essay-based such as history or politics. However, my parents suggested that I might enjoy the work placements that I was due to take later in the year at the *Sunderland Echo* and Century Radio in Gateshead. After deciding that such a change would be difficult to go through with, I decided to stay with journalism.

Elsewhere, I was starting to read *Living Marxism* very enthusiastically. As well as helping me (to an extent) with essay writing, I also found that it provided an antidote to the politically correct way that issues in current affairs were often presented in newspapers and on television, as well as the way that they were taught by journalism lecturers. Much of *Living Marxism*'s content was anti-establishment and very politically incorrect. I found out about a *Living Marxism* readers group based in Newcastle and started to attend meetings, where issues covered in the magazine were discussed. I really enjoyed these meetings.

Later, I attended a conference organized by *Living Marxism* where I developed new special interests, including the conflict in the former Yugoslavia, which would later provide me with a topic of future study. I feel that I learned more from this experience than being stuck in a classroom being instructed to write for an audience. At the conference, I felt as though I was able to express my opinions about different issues much more easily. It wasn't long before I had to go back to university and into what I felt was a more closed and exclusive environment where I wasn't wanted.

Pushed into a corner

At the end of my first term, it was time for me to undertake my work placements. Before my placements, I initially thought that in a working environment, I might learn more by actually doing it rather than sitting in a classroom. When I started my placement at the *Sunderland Echo* I found it very difficult to relate the college-based training that I had received to a working newsroom. Previously, I had done my school work experience there, but this involved shadowing journalists at different events at places such as the local magistrates court, council chamber and so on. This time though, I was left on my own and expected to be able to go out into the town and come back with something. This made me feel very confused as I didn't know where to go or what to do, especially as it wasn't made clear as to what I was supposed to come back with. I was also encouraged by the news editor to think of some ideas that may be useful. But really, this meant putting me to one side out of the way as if they couldn't be bothered with me.

What particularly intimidated me within the environment of the newsroom was not only the noise but also that everybody who worked there seemed to have his or her own agenda or ambition and had the 'I want to beat you' mentality. It was clear that they didn't have any time for someone like me, who didn't know where he was going.

After the *Sunderland Echo*, I moved on to Century Radio, which was worse. When they saw that I lacked any initiative and couldn't settle in quickly, they made it clear that they didn't want me to experience being part of things, pushing me to one side again. Something that I found out from my work placements is that journalism is highly competitive field. I didn't initially realise the extent of it until I found that media organisations receive so many CVs per week from people wanting to be reporters or DJs and that it was a lottery if you were to make it. It appeared that you were either what they were looking for or if not, they didn't want to know you and you were wasting their time. At Century Radio, the news editor even told me that I wasn't cut out for a career in broadcasting.

Visit to Russia

After the unpleasantness that I experienced on my placements, I felt that I needed a holiday. By now, at 19 years old, I was developing a desire to travel and felt that I had hardly even got beyond my front door. The interest in Russian history that I had developed from my modern history lectures was encouraging me to visit Moscow. I didn't have a friend to go with and my parents were concerned about me going to Moscow on my own, so my father decided that he would come with me. I didn't mind, as after all, I was going to visit a different country, something which then, I didn't get much opportunity to do.

Looking into tours, I found an appropriate city break in Moscow, which included a guided tour given by a tour guide. In Moscow, I visited the Kremlin, where our guide introduced us to its collections. What I particularly wanted to see though was Lenin's Mausoleum in Red Square, where visitors could file past the embalmed body of Vladimir Lenin.

My visit to Russia did me good as I felt I learned much more from travelling than being stuck in a classroom. When I got back home, my parents, after noticing that I had enjoyed my Moscow visit, pushed me to look for a summer job so that I could perhaps start saving up for another visit abroad. But after what I felt I had experienced on my work placements, I didn't feel confident enough to be able to look for work.

8

Difficult Days:
My Second Year at University

When I arrived back at university to start the second year of my course, there were many changes taking place that, although I had been informed of them at the end of my first year, I was very anxious about, as I didn't know what to expect. The anxiety was making me feel very stressed about going back. The changes involved different course content and a change of course leadership.

For my second year, I changed accommodation. Again, I was in a rented room, but this time it was self-catering, for which I had my own kitchen facilities as well as laundry facilities. There was another student who rented a room in the property, Ruth, from Skelmersdale. At first, I thought that the self-catering arrangement would provide me with more flexibility, but it proved very difficult for me to get used to, as I had been used to the more rigid routine of set meal times.

Difficulties with lecturers

At university, much of the course content changed. New modules that I had to do were Media Law and Newspaper Production. Previously, I had thought that the idea of higher education was that nobody would make you learn, but the lecturer that I had for Media Law was more like a school teacher. My colleagues liked her non-nonsense approach, but as far as I was concerned, the way that she 'enforced' her subject on students was a discouragement for me to study. For Newspaper Production, a new lecturer was appointed who also had a tyrant mentality about her.

These two lecturers made my life difficult. My Media Law lecturer often accused me of not taking notes during lectures and not taking part during seminars. I felt that I had much to say at the seminars, but each time I kept trying to say something, she felt that my contribution was irrelevant. Meanwhile, my Newspaper Production lecturer kept accusing me of holding back the class. She thought that I wasn't working hard enough, not realising that I was a slow developer and needed more attention. It didn't help when she kept reminding me that others were already much further ahead of me 'at this stage' and that I didn't have any hope of getting anywhere with journalism. This lowered my self-esteem. Elsewhere, my lecturer for government didn't know his subject and rather than teaching it, he just read it all out of a textbook. I found this a particular insult.

The journalism lecturers only seemed interested in working with the more ambitious career-minded students, rather than those who needed their attention the most, such as myself. They kept blaming me for holding back the class, but I knew that I was falling behind because they couldn't be bothered to give me the extra attention that I perhaps could have done with. They were probably just trying to get me to leave the course by making me feel that they couldn't be bothered with me.

Difficulties with colleagues

As well as not getting on with some of the lecturers, I also found it increasingly difficult to interact with other students. They were very career-minded and ambitious and didn't have time for somebody like myself who worried too much and seemed 'lost'. I was becoming plagued with worry, not realising what others thought of me. Many of them, unlike me, had been successful at their placements and some had even been offered jobs or had at least been invited back. In this way, I felt that I was almost expected to be in a job before completing the course. I found that I couldn't relate to career-minded conversations and I noticed that 'exclusive' groups of students were forming. To me, this seemed like an attempt to deter the likes of myself. Also, when visiting speakers came, they accused me of being an embarrassment to the class by asking questions that they thought were stupid, but I thought were relevant.

Feeling unable to interact with anybody around me and not being involved, I found myself going home back to Sunderland every weekend. Things weren't too much better at home either as my sister was suffering from Body Dismorphic Disorder (BDD) and my brother wasn't happy with his 'A' levels at college. When they saw that I wasn't happy at college either, my parents were now wondering where they had gone wrong with all three of us. Most weekends, I found myself being faced with only two choices of what to do – it was either stay in Darlington on my own or go back home where things weren't much better. At least at home I had the security of my family around me.

Imbalanced self-esteem

It wasn't all doom and gloom as there was a new module that I had grown to like, Media Issues, taught by Phillip Cass, whose lectures I really enjoyed.

Not only was he knowledgeable about his subject, he was also entertaining as a lecturer! Media Issues was more academic than the practical journalism workshops that I really disliked and looked at the international perspective of media, including different interpretations of foreign policy. I found that I was able to relate my interests in Politics and Modern History to this module.

For the main part though, I was becoming increasingly uninterested in my studies and felt as though I was pursuing the wrong subject. I didn't want to be there. I realised that I wasn't training to become a journalist for my own needs but for the expectations of others and that I had had a false introduction to the profession of journalism through a student newspaper. I also began to realise that many of the journalism lecturers had gone into lecturing either because they got fed up of being journalists or because they hadn't got where they wanted to be within the profession. The only students that they were interested in were those who appeared to be ambitious and that they could see going on to be successful journalists, probably because they (the lecturers) didn't achieve what they wanted to within journalism. As a substitute for what they couldn't achieve, they probably decided to live their lives through their successful students.

Social isolation and comfort eating

I found myself becoming more isolated living in self-catering accommodation, not eating proper meals and snacking on crisps each time I felt hungry. I started to lose weight very quickly. Indeed my mother noticed that I had got thinner since going back to start my second year at university. Soon though, the snacking became comfort eating as I was becoming depressed. As I became depressed, I started feeling very angry and was shutting myself off from everything else around me. In my room, I was starting to rediscover my interest in heavy metal music, as I found myself being able to relate to its angry, aggressive sound. I found that some of Guns N' Roses' lyrics provided appropriate messages for people whom I felt were making my lives a misery. One of Guns N' Roses tracks, 'It's so Easy', had an appropriate message for my Media Law and Newspaper Production lecturers:

> 'I see you standing there, you think you're so cool, why don't you just, FUCK OFF!'

I started to self-harm, often by cutting myself with a razor blade because I was so angry. My colleagues began to notice some of the marks on my arms. At first, they wondered if I had been attacked, but I kept replying that it was my cat that had made the scratches. Also, my colleagues noticed that I had become thinner. At the property where I lived, my landlady noticed that there was something unusual about my behaviour and that I was different to most other students who had previously been there. She noticed that I was spending much more time in my room by myself than what she had been used to with other students that she had taken in. Ruth, the other student who lived in the property, noticed blood on the sink in the bathroom, suggesting that I had been self-harming.

When my parents found out about what I was going through, they decided that it would be better for me to come back home for the rest of the term where I would feel more secure. By then, I had started making cuts in more visible places, including on my face. By now, they realised that I wasn't happy and needed help, so they got me to a doctor. Back at university, my colleagues noticed that I wasn't around and became worried about what had happened to me. At this point, my colleagues started to become more concerned for me.

Brave new world?

The first person to contact me after I went back home was Myles Ashby. He said that everybody back at college now felt guilty that I had become socially isolated from everybody else and they would be sorry if I had to leave. I also received another phone call from a Norwegian student, Geir Sabel, who had been concerned that I had quit the course and would miss my input at seminars. The response that I received from my colleagues couldn't have been any better. The course reps, Claire Dunwell and Emma Kingswood arranged for a get well soon card to be signed by everybody. The card contained all kinds of great messages.

After the encouraging response that I received from my colleagues, I started to feel much better in myself, although I still wasn't quite well enough to return. The course leader, Philip Cass, had heard about what had happened and offered me mitigating circumstances for some of the assignments that I had missed.

It was during this time that I found out that my mother had kept articles from newspapers and magazines about Asperger's syndrome, a form of autism, that she thought I might have and that explained why I was the way I was. I had never heard of this condition and neither had my doctor. However, after reading some literature about the condition from the National Autistic Society's website, I found that some of the characteristics, particularly special interests, difficulty in being able to think abstractly, my liking for routine and difficulty of being able to handle unpredictable situations applied to me. In parts it seemed like a description of my personality. I also read a book by

Dr Tony Attwood about Asperger's syndrome, which in parts, I thought was almost as if it was written about myself, especially the childhood obsession with *Thomas the Tank Engine and Friends* and the ability to memorise sports commentary.

I was nearly 20 years old and I was just finding out why I was the way I was and possibly the most important and most defining part of who I am. My life was never going to be the same again, but in a more positive sense. The next step was obtaining a diagnosis.

'Australia' (2000) shows me with Garry's young adults group in Brisbane. Anti-clockwise from back is Peter Bielby, Chris Innes, Garry Burge, Damian Donovan, John Gibbs and myself.

Glass Half Full

9

It All Becomes Clear:
My Asperger's Syndrome Diagnosis

Discovering that I might have Asperger's syndrome provided me with an opportunity to review my life, looking at why I had handled events in my life the way I had. For example, I realised why I had found it very difficult to make friends at school, why I had been clumsy at playing sport and why I was, at times, a slow developer academically. I also realised why, in the past, my parents were concerned about me spending too much time by myself in my room and not playing with others my age. As much as I didn't like their interventions to try and make me more like other kids when young, I don't blame them for this as I now realise that they were just trying to help. When I was younger, I also realised that there might be a reason for how obsessive I often was in terms of my behaviour, such as repeatedly drawing rainbows, which apparently lasted almost a year.

Additionally, I found out about some things from my past that I never previously knew about. I didn't realise that in primary school, it had been suggested by an educational psychologist that I may have Asperger's syndrome, but back then, there wasn't a diagnosis available. Also, I found out that when five years old, I had been offered a place at a special school for children with autism, but the head teacher at Rickleton Primary School didn't want me to go in case I became institutionalised. As a result, I remained in mainstream education throughout my life.

Assessing myself

Understanding that I may have Asperger's syndrome also gave me a chance to make my own assessment of my strengths and weaknesses, which I hadn't felt that I had the chance to do before making important decisions and transitions during my life, such as with university and careers. I was weak at handling unpredictability and pressure, things that I felt very uncomfortable with during my work placements. At university, I felt very uncomfortable with having to put up with so many course changes, in particular, the constant changes of exam dates that I had been through. Another of my weaknesses that I was able to recognise was my inability to make friends easily and also my inability to have a reciprocal conversation. I would so often steer conversation topics onto subjects that I felt I had a lot of knowledge on and that I liked to repeat, not often knowing what others felt of me (most likely that I was rather boring).

I also looked at the strengths that I felt that the condition gave me. One of these was my often remarkable memory, something that I had been complimented on many times. It was something that other people around me even envied, particularly because as well as being able to remember football and cricket facts and figures, I could remember when different people's birthdays were as well as word for word what I had heard in lectures, films and television. So many people have told me that they would love to have a memory as good as mine.

The other positive abilities that the condition presented me with were the ability to specialise and an eye for detail. I often found that I was able to remember even the smallest detail of what I had seen so well. Other people may find such detail boring, but I am often able to pick out the relevance of even the smallest detail in a film or story, even if I sometimes can't understand the plot involved at first. I would specialise in subjects such as railways or astronomy. often to the extent where I would become so focused on a particular interest that other people may have thought that I was either 'sad' or 'boring', but I felt that I had something to keep me occupied and interested, whereas other people may need to have active social lives so that they have something to talk about.

Obtaining a diagnosis

While recovering from my depression, I was referred to a psychiatrist based in Sunderland. At the appointment, I initially hoped that I might be able to find out where I could obtain an Asperger's syndrome diagnosis, but it turned out to be a difficult experience. The psychiatrist very quickly dismissed any idea that I might have Asperger's syndrome and that I could not be diagnosed on past behaviour. I found the whole set-up intimidating as rather than sitting in an open environment, I sat on the opposite side of a desk. Together with the, at times, forceful way that he asked me questions, I felt it was more like a police interview. I later realised that he might have been trying to write a paper rather than actually help me and was asking me questions in this way so that he could get the answers he wanted rather than listen to how I actually felt.

After the unpleasantness of this appointment, my parents and I looked around for places from where I could obtain a diagnosis. Realising that it wasn't going to be possible to obtain a diagnosis from the National Health Service, we decided to go private. The National Autistic Society provided us with an address of Estelle Louw, a consultant psychologist based in Chester-le-Street, County Durham, who could give an Asperger's syndrome diagnosis.

What I found out about myself from my diagnosis

At my diagnosis, so much came up about my upbringing that I never previously knew about. For instance, I didn't realise that my mother had a kidney infection for the last three weeks of her pregnancy and had been treated for high blood pressure. At the time of my birth, I had two cardiac arrests.

Although, I had been able to walk at ten months, during my developmental phase I often reacted badly to changes such as being moved from cot to bed. From such a dislike of change, my parents thought that I was rather different, especially after they later saw how my brother and sister didn't have many problems with such changes. My medical history was largely uneventful apart from frequent earaches during which grommets were inserted into my ears four times.

I said my first words very early. At about 18 months, I used echolalia, nonsensically repeating what I had heard my parents or relatives say or what I had heard on television. Two names that I repeated from what I had heard on television were 'Bamber Gascoigne' and 'Peter Sissons'. My parents were, and still are, keen watchers of University Challenge. While I was growing up, I apparently used to repeat the name 'Bamber Gascoigne' each time the programme started. When the news came on, I used to repeat the name 'Peter Sissons'. My early communication was described as egocentric, as in I wasn't able to respond to others, but I used my own words and phrases, of which the meaning wasn't always clear to others, who were often baffled as to what context I was saying such words in.

Catalogue of social isolation

It was noted that I felt social isolation in different settings in my life including Rickleton Primary School, Fulwell Juniors, Monkwearmouth Comprehensive, Monkwearmouth College and most recently, the University of Teesside. I often felt frustrated about other people needing to be in gangs at school or at university –'exclusive groups' – while I didn't understand what this was about. As an individual, I often felt happy with the way I was and didn't feel as though I needed to act or dress a particular way just to be acceptable to other people. Even when I did appear to be part of a group or cult, such as when I was a mosher, I still didn't fit in socially.

My assessment also noted that I had not developed social relationships appropriate to my cognitive level, not spontaneously seeking to share social enjoyment with other people as well as lacking social and emotional reciprocity. Lacking in reciprocity, I felt that I had very fixed views on issues such as politics and often found other people's opinions very hard to understand, especially when there isn't a right or wrong answer. What was also noted was that while I was able to express myself and understand others, I often listened and responded in a specific and perceptive framework, putting limitations on my capacity to both understand and express myself. This was often a problem in class discussions at school and seminars at university, particularly when my point of view was challenged. When being able to express my point of view, I was often able to plan what I was going to say, but when questioned, I had to be able to respond 'on the spot' without being able to plan and structure an appropriate answer.

My defining characteristic

Unlike the psychiatrist, Mrs Louw actually talked to me rather than at me and, from this, I felt able to talk about what I had been going through both currently and previously. The conclusion of my assessment suggested that my diagnosis was Asperger's syndrome rather than high-level autism. I was 20 years old and I experienced what I feel is the most defining moment in my life to date. I finally had a name, or a characteristic, for who I am. Prior to my diagnosis, I had felt that my life had been a chronic failure and hadn't achieved anything. However, because I didn't previously know who I was or why I was the way I was, I felt that I had to live up to society's expectations. I now realised that I had initially managed well to stay in mainstream school during my school life and, even though I was having problems with my degree at university, I realised that I had initially done well enough to get into university without any specialist help.

Now though, due to my age, none of the specialist educational support systems were available to me. Mrs Louw contacted Lynne Moxon, a Chartered Psychologist based at European Services for People with Autism (ESPA) in Sunderland. Lynne, who has since played a major role in my development as an adult after my diagnosis, asked me if I would like to take part in classes with other students with Asperger's syndrome at ESPA. This provided me with my first opportunity to meet others diagnosed with Asperger's syndrome, who had experienced things similar to what I had just been through.

One of the reasons why Lynne Moxon felt that my presence at classes would be beneficial was because as I had managed to get into university without specialist help, I could perhaps show other students what could be achieved. This sounded very rewarding to me, especially if it meant other people with Asperger's syndrome being able to avoid having to go through some of the difficulties that I had been through. Attending classes on 'Aspects of Adulthood', I found that much of the content was about real life situations and social conventions. Although it was very basic, I felt that at my age I was old enough to appreciate it and at times I found parts of it quite entertaining. My attendances at these classes did my self-esteem much good and I soon felt confident enough to go back to university.

10

My Return to University and Graduation:
An Achievement Against the Odds

Before going back to university, there were still issues I felt I had to consider, such as what I would do with my qualification. My ambitions had changed since my Asperger's syndrome diagnosis and I had reviewed my strengths and weaknesses. I no longer wanted to be a journalist as I had become so disappointed by the industry. I felt it had promised much in terms of a fulfilling career, but it had let me down very badly. What disappointed me most about the industry was the lack of consistency in terms of recruitment, in that it wasn't clear as to what experience and qualifications was required. The other aspect that I didn't like about the newspaper industry was being surrounded by ambitious colleagues who wanted to progress, often at your expense. This made the whole environment feel like a professional wild west, with pen-slingers out to get you. However, after a visit to the careers office at Sunderland University, I found out that there was a wide range of postgraduate courses that I could do if I could obtain my degree. Knowing that I could apply for postgraduate courses if I could obtain at least a 2:1, provided me with a new motive to study.

Welcome back

When I went back to university for my final year, I received a warm welcome from my colleagues who were pleased to see me again. They even arranged a quiet welcome back party for me, which was really nice. This welcome enabled me to bury some of the differences of opinion that I had with some of them and it later helped us to make the best of what was to be our last year together. From then on, they made real efforts to include me in the social scene of university life, something that I had really missed out on up to now. For instance, they invited me to 21st birthday parties or asked me to come along to a pub or to the Students Union bar. This made me feel much more included. I also felt it necessary to tell some of my colleagues that I had been diagnosed with Asperger's syndrome, especially Myles and Geir and the course reps, Claire and Emma.

For my final year of undergraduate study, I lived at home in Sunderland, where I felt much more secure. To travel to Teesside each day, my parents helped me with buying my first car, a 1992 Nissan Micra. Rather than going around garages and being pressured by car salesmen, I bought it from a local mechanic, who is a good friend of the family. Although I had initially passed my test at the third attempt when 18-years-old, I had driven very little since. So that I felt able to complete the 25-mile per day journey to Teesside, my driving instructor Bill very kindly gave me some in-house top-up lessons. Bill was a fantastic instructor and I got on really well with him. I couldn't have got through my test if it hadn't been for him.

Special arrangements

At the start of my third year, I found that the content was much more optional, so I could take subjects that I had liked studying such as European History and International Relations. This enabled me to shape my studies so that I would be able to create a routine for myself with more predictability. As I started my final year, I began to feel much more settled than I had been able to in my first or second years.

My tutors, Philip Cass and Adrian Quinn, were also informed that I had been diagnosed with Asperger's syndrome. They read up on what they could about the condition and with my co-operation, they worked out some strategies to help me in my studies such as arranging for me to have access to a student counsellor, which was a great help. One of my weaknesses that I had identified since my diagnosis was that I often had difficulty being able to grasp the gestalts of particular themes of study. To help me with this, it was arranged for me to have study skills sessions at the learning resource centre with a learning support assistant. I had also had great difficulty being able to sit exams during my first and second years, not because I couldn't answer the questions appropriately, but because I couldn't handle the pressure of being able to complete the paper within the allocated time, so it was arranged for me by my student counselor to have 25 per cent extra time at exams. With these special arrangements the quality of my work became much better and my grades were on a par with others.

Specialisation ability

One of the strengths that I had identified after my diagnosis was my ability to be able to specialise. This was an advantage for when I started my dissertation. For my dissertation, I decided to study the media coverage of the conflict in the former Yugolsavia, after I had saved some notes and other documentation from the Living Marxism conference two years earlier.

When pursuing my dissertation, I also arranged to have regular meetings with Philip Cass, who was to be my dissertation supervisor. He developed a good understanding of Asperger's syndrome and having previously taught in different countries and to different cultures, I found his input very beneficial. His experience of being able to relate to different cultures with different values helped him to understand me better. With my newfound confidence, I was becoming very studious in my work and was really beginning to enjoy my studies, being able to take a much more calm and patient approach, without the stress or worry that had previously plagued me. Very quickly, I was becoming immersed in my dissertation.

The more I was enjoying my studies during my final year, the happier I was and the more confident I became. Outside of university, I also rediscovered some of the pastimes that I had so enjoyed when younger, including astronomy and model railways. In some cases, I even found that my rediscovery of these hobbies reinforced some of my assignments. For example, I based one of my radio assignments on the potential re-opening of a disused railway line in County Durham. I found that where I was able to apply my special interests to my studies, I could obtain some very high grades.

Socially, I was fitting in much better with my colleagues. After my diagnosis, one of the aspects of social interaction that I felt I needed to work on was being able to have a reciprocal conversation with others. By now, I was beginning to learn how to respect other people's opinions, even those I disagreed with. One of the habits I began to develop when conversing with others about subjects such as football was asking how they felt about a particular refereeing decision or whom they thought should be in the England squad, before expressing my own opinion.

Happier than expected outcome

At the end of term, my course reps Claire and Emma asked me if I would like to attend the annual ball. Previously, I had never been too keen on such parties, especially as I had felt out of place at such events and didn't like drinking alcohol. However, this time was different, as it was the last time that we would all be together before graduation, and after the way that they had initially welcomed me back, I felt obliged to attend. Unlike other such events I had been to, there was a required dress code for the ball, which involved having to wear a tuxedo. Myles helped me with hiring a tuxedo, which I thought felt uncomfortable, but I would only need to wear for one night. It turned out to be a great night and I felt that I had made up for what I felt I had missed out on over the last three years.

My grades from my final year, in particular the grade I received for my dissertation (a first), helped to increase my eventual degree grade. I received a 2:1, which at one time, especially during my second year, didn't seem possible, especially after I came so close to quitting. But it showed me what I was capable of achieving once the necessary adaptations were made. My tutors and support workers were so pleased that it had worked out and felt that my grade was well deserved, especially after all the research I had done for my dissertation and the work that I had put in during my final year. It is quite possible, and I still sometimes feel that if I had the special arrangements from earlier on, I could have even attained a first, but I was more than happy with a 2:1, as it enabled me to apply to study at postgraduate level.

After starting university with what I now feel were false and unrealistic ambitions and expectations, I now came out a very different person, knowing who I actually was after my Asperger's syndrome diagnosis. As my colleagues went away to start their careers in the media, I found myself unsure and confused about what to do or where to go next.

11

Finding My Niche:
My Way into Work and Postgraduate Study

When coming out of university, I found myself faced with a very uncertain immediate future. I had obtained a journalism degree that I felt I couldn't use in a practical way, particularly after I had discovered that a career in journalism wasn't for me. Although I wanted to pursue postgraduate study, I still wasn't sure what courses to apply for and felt that I needed to obtain some actual employment experience before applying to do any further study, something that, at 21 years old, I had never had.

When signing on to receive unemployment benefit while looking for a job, I was advised to buy *The Evening Chronicle*, a local newspaper every Thursday, when jobs were advertised. At first, when I started applying for jobs, I requested application forms for just about every job that was advertised that I thought that I could do and to what my qualifications closely matched, on the basis of what the advert said. I didn't realise that many of the jobs that I applied to were more interested in experience relevant to the post advertised rather than qualifications. As I didn't have any employment experience at all other than work placements, I often found myself having to leave sections of applications blank, which I didn't realise would be a waste of an application and that as soon as such gaps were seen, the form would be dismissed.

Finding support

For over two months after leaving university, I had applied for over fifty jobs, which I didn't realise that I had had no hope of getting. At the time, I became very frustrated, not understanding why I wasn't hearing from any of the posts that I had applied to. Feeling that I needed help with applying for jobs, I contacted Prospects, the National Autistic Society's supported employment scheme, but as I lived outside London, they couldn't offer much help.

Later, I made an appointment to see a Disability Employment Advisor (DEA) at my local job centre in Sunderland. From the advice I received, I found out where I had been going wrong with my applications. I hadn't been filling in application forms the way they were supposed to be filled in. When I first started filling in job application forms, I felt that the purpose of them was for the applicant to express him/herself about their personality and interests rather than showing how skills, experience and qualifications related to the post applied for. I found out what I was supposed to do when filling in an application form – use the person specification and job description provided as a guide.

After I found out how to fill in application forms appropriately, I was shortlisted for interview for the position of clerical assistant with North Tyneside District Council. As I had never been to a job interview before, I didn't know what to expect, so I arranged to have a mock interview with my DEA. The actual interview though was very different to the mock interview as I was before a panel of three interviewers, whereas at the mock interview I had just been in with my DEA. Having to adjust eye contact to focus on each member of the panel was difficult. I also had great difficulty being able to structure an answer to each question, often making pauses. At face value, this didn't look good.

Do I mention it?

Another problem I had when applying for jobs was that I wasn't sure whether to mention on my application that I had Asperger's syndrome. My DEA made an appointment for me to see an occupational psychologist. I asked the occupational psychologist if it would be worth mentioning in my applications that I had Asperger's syndrome. He said that it wouldn't be necessary and firms might discriminate against applicants who didn't have a condition classified as a disability. This at first made me think that if I did include it on application forms, my application may be dismissed immediately.

The occupational psychologist also suggested that it might be an idea to undertake voluntary work while looking for a paid position or register with employment agencies. I had had little luck with applications and didn't feel comfortable at the interview stage, so I registered with several agencies. One of these agencies managed to find me some part-time temporary work doing data entry for a marketing firm. The agency expected me to start the post within four hours. This was a shock and I wasn't sure how to react. As it was an opportunity for paid employment, I felt that I had to take it but felt very stressed about having to locate the firm and find my way there within such a short time.

When I started this post, which was my first paid employment, I had to settle in very quickly. First days at work are rough for most people, but I had to get used to the role as if I had been doing it for a few months with little training. When inputting data, I tried to do it as accurately as possible, not realising that speed was just as important. I wasn't given any idea of how many entries I was supposed to make in a day. The supervisor was at first impressed with my accuracy, but when she noticed that my total inputted was considerably below the requirement, she became furious and said that I had cost so much to take on and hadn't produced anything in return. This sudden change frightened me, as I wasn't aware of any targets. The supervisor then accused me of lying on my application form, but it turned out that the agency had placed me in a position that was supposed to be for an applicant who had passed the appropriate data entry speed test. As a result, my first job was terminated and I felt very hard done by, being placed in a position that wasn't suitable.

Closed shop

After my first job was cut short, I now felt it necessary to mention on application forms that I had Asperger's syndrome. I felt it was necessary for potential employers to know, in case I had difficulty being able to adapt to my place of work. Although I was occasionally short-listed for interview, at the interview I often found that I couldn't put what I wanted to say into words and, through bad nerves, I often found that my body language became very mixed up, especially my hand movements.

I managed to find a way round this barrier by registering with agencies where I was tested in terms of skills before being placed in a position. Whereas at interviews, I felt that I was being seen at face value before the employer had a chance to see how eager I was to work hard, with an agency, my ability could be measured first to see which positions I would perhaps be best suited. It also meant that when placed in a position, there would be a period where I could get used to the place of work and the agency's client company could get used to me. However, most work offered by the employment agencies was temporary, which made being made permanent in an organisation seem like a 'closed shop' to me, especially since I felt I couldn't get through a job interview.

Preference for routine

Eventually, one of the agencies found me a position in a college library in Sunderland to cover for a member of staff on long-term illness. Unlike my work placements, I found this post much easier to settle into as it was a much slower-paced environment. This allowed for more predictability in my role, which helped to reduce stress.

What I liked about the library was the order and structure of its content and the way it was organised. I quickly managed to get used to the Dewey Decimal system when shelving books and it wasn't long before I knew which Dewey Decimal numbers related to particular subjects by memory. As a library assistant, much of my responsibilities were very basic. Whereas some may see such tasks as rather mundane and lacking in excitement, I liked them, as I felt that I had difficulty being able to cope with the unpredictability of pressure. This position showed me that I was better suited to roles that involved structure and routine more than those that involved pressure. Through the staff at the City of Sunderland College, I found out about available postgraduate courses, one of which was conveniently located near home. This was a Masters in Information and Library Management at the University of Northumbria at Newcastle (UNN).

As my position was temporary, it ended after five months when the member of staff whom I was brought in to cover for returned. My supervisor provided me with a reference when applying for a place on UNN's postgraduate librarianship course. The practical experience that I had gained working in a library was of great use for my application to postgraduate study.

12

Re-inventing Myself:
Postgraduate Study

It wasn't long before I found out that I was accepted for a place on the Masters at UNN. However, the next step was being able to find the funding to be able to pursue the course.

Form confusion

The university considered me for a bursary award and I had to request a bursary application form from the Arts and Humanities Research Board (AHRB). When logging on to the AHRB's website to download a form, I found that there were many different forms available and I wasn't sure which one that I was supposed to request for the type of award I was eligible to apply for.

The form that I accessed was quite complicated to fill in and had to be typed up rather than written by hand. However, I found out that the form I had filled in was the wrong form. It was complicated to fill in because it was supposed to be for applicants pursuing research-orientated studies rather than taught postgraduate courses. So I found myself having to rewrite a different form. I very nearly missed the application deadline date courtesy of this confusion.

When filling in my application form, I put forward my reasoning for why I felt that I needed the qualification. I now felt it necessary to mention on my job application forms that I had Asperger's syndrome. I mentioned that I had the condition in my application for a bursary award, suggesting that I needed a qualification that was related to a career where I could use my condition as a strength. After what I had experienced at the City of Sunderland College library, some of the advantages that Asperger's syndrome provided me with for a career in this field included my need for structure, routine and predictability as well as my eye for detail and memory.

However, what I also had to be aware of was that competition for such awards was fierce. In case my bursary application was unsuccessful, I had to explore other possible sources of funding, especially as the tuition fees for the course were over £2,500, which I didn't have. One of the sources that I looked into was a career development loan, available for vocational courses connected to a career. Finding that career development loans would have to be paid back within a year of completing the course, I was put off by this idea, especially since I already had student loans from my undergraduate study that I couldn't repay.

Back to university

Fortunately, I was later informed that my application for a bursary had been successful, so I didn't need to pay any fees. Additionally, I was provided with a maintenance grant for the year. Going back to university, I felt that I had a chance to make up for what I had been through as an undergraduate. At Teesside, I felt that I wasn't studying journalism for myself but for the expectations of others, but this time I knew that I had selected the course that I wanted to study, as librarianship/information management was a field where I felt I could contribute effectively. Since my Asperger's syndrome diagnosis, I felt that I was able to assess my own strengths and weaknesses rather than letting others do it for me.

My diagnosis also meant I knew when I needed learning support. This time, special arrangements could be made from the start. I had mentioned on my application form that I had Asperger's syndrome, so when I started postgraduate study I had a meeting with my personal tutor where we discussed arrangements that I may benefit from. One of these was being able to make regular appointments with my module tutors before handing in assignments so I knew if the content that I had included was relevant and that the writing style I had used was appropriate. If not I would be able to alter it before handing it in for marking. I also felt that it would be necessary for my colleagues to know that I had Asperger's syndrome, especially as the course involved a significant amount of group work.

Tolerance

At the start of my course, I met the other students with whom I would be studying. The course leaders arranged a day out to Grassmere in the Lake District, the home of the poet William Wordsworth. This was a good way for me to get to know other people in what was a leisurely atmosphere. One of the aspects of postgraduate study that I liked was that rather than being among a group largely made up of people aged around 18-19 away from home for the first time, I was around a group of people of different disciplines, backgrounds and some from different cultures and faiths. As my postgraduate colleagues were all graduates of many different subjects ranging from Theology to Biochemistry, I found the atmosphere much more open and accepting. In an environment where the range of topics of conversation was wider and more open and experience being rather varied, I felt that I could be myself more around others. This made me much more confident about getting to know other students.

Many of the students that I got to know well were, like myself, very individual in terms of character. One of the first people that I got to know was Steve Lancaster, who was later voted course rep. I felt able to tell Steve that I had Asperger's syndrome and I was surprised when I found that he knew what it was! Steve had come across Asperger's syndrome as he had read Donna Williams' first book *Nobody Nowhere*. I was so pleased to meet someone who knew of Asperger's syndrome. A keen artist in his spare time, Steve had an imagination to which I could relate well. Another student whom I met who had individual character that I could relate to was Sarah Jenkin. Sarah also had a special interest to which I could relate. She was devoted to the British television programme *The Prisoner* that ran for one series and hosted a website and E-mailing list about it. I could relate so well to such a special interest and she liked my ability to be able to specialise in television programmes, being able to remember quotes, especially *The Simspons*, which by now had become my favourite show.

Other students with whom I could relate to well were those from different cultures and different faiths. As a university student with Asperger's syndrome, I felt that I was often able to relate well to overseas students. It is understandable that a student with Asperger's syndrome in most situations might feel like someone trying to find their way round a country that spoke a different language. As I felt that I had experienced this when an undergraduate student before diagnosis, I could understand what the foreign students may be going through when trying to find their way around an English-speaking university.

The social environment among postgraduate students was very different to what I experienced as an undergraduate. Social activity among postgraduate students rarely involved wild nights and drinking and instead, much activity involved going for walks in the Northumberland countryside and quiet social get-togethers. I found this much more welcoming and less intimidating in terms of noise. This enabled me to feel even more confident about getting to know others.

Work placement

Another element of the course content that was useful was the supervised placement that I did at Gateshead Local Studies Centre. As well as my placement being supervised, there was also another student from the course who did a placement there, Catherine Warner. Like Steve and Sarah, Catherine also did much to include me in social events and it was really good to have somebody around whom I knew, so I didn't feel that I was 'on my own'. The placements that I had done when an undergraduate student were not supervised, so the employers could just push me out of the way in the corner. UNN, however, had kept a list of placements where previous students had worked and who felt that they had learned something in a practical environment. Places where students felt that they had been pushed aside were removed from the list and future students were advised not to apply to such places. A supervised placement, I felt, would give me a chance to find out how effective I was as an employee and which areas I could perhaps improve in.

When arranging my placement, I found that there were a lot of options available in terms of partner organisations that the university had, in a wide variety of library/information management roles, including specialisms. One of these specialisms that really appealed to me was local history. This was something that I had developed a passion in through my interest in railways. When seeing a picture of a railway station, I often found myself able to see more than just a railway station, such as the town it served and what the railway brought in and out of the town. Also, when looking at pictures of local landmarks (for example, lighthouses, bridges, churches and so on), I was often able to see much history that applied to it. For instance, when seeing a picture of a bridge across the River Tyne in Newcastle, I was able to see more than just an architectural structure, as I could see the places that it linked (Newcastle and Gateshead) and what the link enabled (growth of businesses along the river).

I was able to put this interest to good effect during my placement at Gateshead Local Studies Centre. I really enjoyed the tasks that I was given to do, which involved developing webpages about local places in and around Gateshead. My favourite aspect of these tasks was researching information in the centre's reference collection in both books and documents (for example, census returns, public health reports). It was a role in which I felt that my eye for detail was really beneficial, especially when describing photographs/images.

Academic progress

As well as being able to fit in socially, I could also handle the assignments well and I learned new and useful skills, including public speaking using Microsoft Powerpoint. Previously, I was often nervous about such situations, particularly when speaking in front of an audience. However, when using Powerpoint, I felt I had what was not only an effective visual aid for the audience, but also effective for me in that I had something to help me keep to the point of what I was supposed to be talking about. I also found that the use of imagery helped to illustrate points that I was attempting to make very well.

What I found so good about the course was that the lecturers were very enthusiastic about their subjects. They could also make what may appear to some as rather boring subjects interesting. One of these subjects was research methods, where I was introduced to effective research methods including ethnography and conducting focus groups. Conducting such research enabled the researcher to be able to back up their findings effectively. These methods, I found, were much more effective than the often arbitrary methods used in media/journalism, which I felt were often invasive, especially door-stepping when looking for a story or looking for quotes that could be interpreted in a way that would sell. My research methods lecturer liked to use visual aids in her lectures, one of which I particularly liked where she showed a cartoon of herself with a beard and moustache in the guise of Ali the Sherpa! By this she meant that she was the sherpa who helped you climb 'Mount Dissertation', 15,000 words high! It was another idiom that I found encouraging.

Social progress and acceptance

There was a lot of group work for many of the modules, particularly Management. Previously, I had found working as part of a team very difficult, but this time I didn't have many problems, as the other students were very tolerant of me, knowing that I had Asperger's syndrome. This, in return, helped me become much more tolerant of others and be able to see my place in a team situation as well as theirs. Unlike at Teesside, I felt that I fitted in much better at UNN, especially as I felt that I could be much better appreciated as an individual among my colleagues.

13

Moving Up:
Finding My First Professional Role

After obtaining my Masters, it was again time for me to look for work. This time I felt I had advantages in terms of being in a position of being able to look for work, unlike when coming out of university as an undergraduate. I now knew which career I wanted to pursue and the qualification that I had obtained, as well as the work placement that I had completed, were relevant to my application.

While applying for jobs, I undertook voluntary work with Durham County Record Office in relation to my interest in local history. My first task at Durham County Record Office was to compile an index of Acts of Parliament relevant to County Durham. The Chief Archivist Jennifer Gill and the Deputy Archivist David Butler were quickly impressed with the speed and accuracy of my work and, above all, my enthusiasm for the subject. After completing this task, I then started compiling an index of soldiers of the Durham Light Infantry killed or wounded during the First World War. Whereas other people may have found such work boring and predictable, I liked the order and routine it involved, and I felt secure in what I was doing, rather than having to meet sudden and unpredictable demands frequently.

Interview barrier

When coming out of university as an undergraduate, I had great difficulty being able to get onto shortlists and had even more difficulty at the interview stage. However, since I had learned how to fill in application forms by relating my personal statement to the job description and person specification, and with my qualification and previous employment relevant to many of the jobs I applied to, I found it much easier this time to get onto shortlists. By now, I made a point of mentioning in job applications that I had Asperger's syndrome. I found that it was especially useful when applying to an organisation that had the Positive About Disabled People quality mark. This meant that if applying to a post where my application form clearly met the requirements in the job description and person specification, the organization had to invite me to an interview. My DEA at my local job centre told me to inform her if I applied to an organisation with this mark where I met the requirements for the post and wasn't selected for interview. If this was the case, the organisation could lose their mark.

For most of the jobs that I applied to, I found that I was able to get onto the shortlist, but there was still a barrier, which was the actual interview itself.

Frustration and perseverance

Whereas the frustration that I felt when I first applying for jobs was that I couldn't get on the shortlist, the frustration this time round was that I couldn't get past the interview stage. When applying for a job on paper, I was able to structure a personal statement relevant to the job as well as being able to include personal qualities. But at interview, I had to be able to provide an appropriate response to questions almost immediately. This resulted in me making many pauses and sometimes going off on a tangent, with the interviewers having to indirectly prompt me to keep to the question. By now, I had also realised the value of gaining feedback from interviews. They often said that, from my answers, they couldn't see how my personal attributes related to the post.

However, I managed to obtain my first paid position since completing my Masters' through a different route. While working at Durham County Record Office, I was in a place where a potential employer could see what I was capable of. I was recommended for a part-time paid position in the Register Office doing a similar task to what I was doing as a volunteer. I was the only male employee but I found that when working with women the environment was very understanding. Working part-time at the Register Office also looked good on my job applications.

Breakthrough!

I was invited for an interview for a position of Assistant Librarian (part-time) at Sunderland University, on a six-month contract covering a maternity leave. Looking at where I had recently went wrong at job interviews, I tried to relate my answers to the questions and this time, when the phone call came through, after I had become so used to be told that I wasn't successful, I was surprised that they offered me the job! After two years, and over thirty attempts, I was finally successful at a job interview! As the post was part-time and the working hours were at weekends and evenings, I was also able to continue my part-time work at the Register Office, so effectively, I was now working full-time with two part-time jobs.

When starting my post at the University of Sunderland's St. Peters' Library, the unusual hours during the evening took a while to get used to, but once I got to know the staff, I felt more comfortable. As Assistant Librarian, my post involved helping with students enquiries and supervising the issue and enquiry desks and being responsible for two other staff members. I found it helpful to talk to the two staff members whom I worked with, as I didn't want them to think I was over-authoritative. Where possible, I also liked to help out with some of the more basic tasks including shelving and tidying, as I didn't want to appear as being 'above' such duties.

A difficulty that I had in my first role in a supervisory capacity was that I was new to the organisation and had to find my way around through all the content as well as getting used to different procedures, such as processing overdue books and notices and inter-library loan requests, but yet I was expected to take charge, managing staff. This was difficult when the two library assistants that I worked with and whose supervisor I was supposed to be had worked at the library for quite a few years and were used to all the procedures that I was learning. As the post was only part-time, it didn't feel continuous. Often, I feel that I need to work long hours so that I am able to get used to the working environment and the tasks. Perhaps if the position was full-time, I could have perhaps settled in quicker and felt more secure in my work, which would have enabled the tasks to have become more routine.

Task imbalance

Although I liked helping students with enquiries, being able to balance this with other tasks that I had to do, such as processing inter-library loans and overdue notices, was often difficult. I could get overloaded when having to do two or more tasks at once. As I was still in the process of learning the procedures, I often had to ask the two library assistants, who knew it better than me, for help when getting stuck. In this way, it appeared as though they were supervising me rather than me supervising them. In this way, I felt I couldn't take charge not only because I was often unsure of myself, but also because I don't consider myself to be an authoritative person or to have any kind of authoritative presence.

This was often a problem when dealing with borrowers complaints. Often in these situations, I had difficulty being able to balance library policy with customer care, especially when it involved payment of fines. Sometimes, when students complained about having to pay fines, I often waived fines to avoid a heated argument, as I could get stressed in this situation. However, the library assistants often reminded me that I shouldn't do this, and often had to remind me that I was supposed to be in charge. Although I tried to assert authority when trying to deal with borrowers complaints, I often found it difficult to refuse requests to waive fines or renew books for students who still had overdue items and it was supposed to be library policy whereby I wasn't supposed to issue items if a borrower had overdue items on his/her card. Often, I found myself giving in to borrowers requests to take out items in this situation when they said that they had deadlines to meet and needed the item badly for just another day.

Although I had worked in a library before, all libraries are different. What I perhaps needed was to experience St Peter's Library from the 'shop floor' as a library assistant so that I could get used to the environment and know what people that I was supervising were doing in terms of duties. Being placed in a supervisory position straight away, I didn't get to see much of this. However, despite my lack of ability to assert authority and my tendency to be too generous with borrowers ahead of library policy, I got on quite well with the staff as I was seen as very approachable.

14

Broadening My Horizons:
Autuniv-1 To Australia, Canada and Back

After my Asperger's syndrome diagnosis, I found out about an e-mailing list for university students and ex-university students with Asperger's syndrome called Autuniv-l, run by Clare Sainsbury, author of *Martian in the Playground* (2000). Although I had met some other people with Asperger's syndrome at classes I attended at ESPA, I felt that I wanted meet others with similar interests and who had been through similar things to what I had been, particularly regarding university experiences. When I first wrote to Clare to ask if she would subscribe me to Autuniv-l, she asked me to submit a personal account about my experiences of being a university student with Asperger's syndrome.

Garry Burge – An Australian mirror image

It wasn't long before I was subscribed and after my personal account was made available on the list, I received my first e-mail from someone who, like me, had just recently been diagnosed with Asperger's syndrome – Garry Burge from Brisbane, Australia. Like me, Garry had recently been diagnosed with Asperger's syndrome and had just completed university. At 26, he was older than I was when I was diagnosed and was finding that although he wanted friends, he had difficulty in forming friendships. He was interested in meeting other people with Asperger's syndrome and starting a group for young adults with the condition.

After receiving a message from Garry, I immediately sent him more information about myself. It was just incredible to converse with someone from the other side of the world who had just experienced similar events to what I had. Garry was the first close friend with Asperger's syndrome that I felt that I had and to whom his experiences I felt I could relate well. It was one of the first times that I realised that I wasn't entirely alone in the world in terms of what I had just been through and that there were other people out there who shared similar experiences.

The more I got to know Garry, the more we wanted to actually meet in person. Garry asked me if I had either been or had ever considered coming to

Australia. After corresponding with him via e-mail, I went beyond the medium of text-based e-mail, corresponding with him by telephone and by postal mail. I found him to be who he was online, so I had a good idea of whom I would be meeting if the opportunity came up.

Correspondence with Tara Kimberley Torme

As the number of subscribers to Autuniv-l grew I came into contact with some new Aspie friends, including Tara Kimberley Torme from Vancouver, Canada. An English Literature graduate, Tara had some interests similar to mine, in particular reading. Like me, she also liked spending time in libraries. In her spare time, she also liked to write poems and posted some of her poems to Autuniv-l when she first subscribed. One of her poems was about Asperger's syndrome, which I really liked. A fluent writer, she often responded to my messages so well and with plenty of detail, which I found very entertaining. As well as similar interests, Tara had also been through some similar events in her school and university life to me, such as bullying and social isolation. She also said that she wanted to meet as many other people diagnosed with Asperger's syndrome as possible.

From our e-mails and from postal and telephone correspondence, I had found that Tara had much in common with me including science-fiction and astronomy. Additionally, we had hobbies that, although we didn't share, we could relate to their therapeutic aspects. For instance, one of Tara's hobbies is embroidery, which to her is very therapeutic, rather like making model buildings is to me.

Long-lost cousins?

Eventually I felt that I wanted to go beyond the limitations of e-mail, telephone and postal communication to meet other people with Asperger's syndrome in person. Garry had encouraged me to visit Australia, a country I thought I would never visit, but the more encouragement I got from his e-mails, the more I wanted to meet him in person. After I had been corresponding with him for a few months, I eventually set out to Australia to meet him.

Garry was waiting for me with his father at Brisbane International Airport. This was the exciting part – it wasn't long before I recognised a face in the group of people waiting at the arrivals point that looked like the picture he had sent me. It was Garry and his father! Garry recognised me straight away from the red and white stripes of my Sunderland AFC shirt, which I'd told him I'd be wearing. It was an incredible moment. For some reason, I already felt I had known him in person for years! He later said that he felt the same about me. When we reached Westlake (where Garry lives), I met his mum, Val Burge, and I gave them their gifts. First, I gave Garry a Sunderland AFC shirt and then gave Tony a City of Sunderland tie and Val a City of Sunderland tea towel. Val said that it was almost like a long-lost family member paying a visit!

It seems very strange, but I felt that I had known Garry and his family all my life. I found that I was able to relate to Garry and what he had been through at University. His parents were also able to relate to me well, as they had been through similar things with Garry to what I had been through with my parents prior to diagnosis. Another thing that Garry said he went through that I could relate to was his relationship with his siblings. Garry is the youngest of four brothers, all of whom are now married and have children and also have good jobs. Understandably, Garry said that he often felt very inferior, as he felt that he could never have any of this. This reminded me of how inferior I felt to my brother who was really good at playing football and other sports, whilst I was hopeless.

Bushwalking

In Australia, I spent a day with an Asperger's syndrome young adults group that Garry had set up in Brisbane. The first person from the group that I met was Damien, who was the same age as me and was very interested in sport. Since leaving high school, Damien had been through a string of temporary positions and spells of unemployment, without ever finding anything permanent. Having recently been through this at home, I could understand where he was coming from.

There were quite a lot of members of the group, which was largely male-dominated. There was one female member who attended the day out who had recently been diagnosed with Asperger's syndrome, Ruth. Ruth was, mentally, a very mixed-up person, as she had had to fend for herself from when very young and prior to eventually being diagnosed with Asperger's syndrome – she had been a prostitute, living rough. I found out how awful the lives of people with Asperger's syndrome can turn out if they don't have the appropriate support from very young and realised how lucky I had been. It was almost as if she had never been given a chance in society and she had almost been destined to live rough from birth. I felt very sorry for what she had been through. It is easy enough for people who don't have Asperger's syndrome to fall out of society, but in the case of Ruth and any other people with Asperger's syndrome who may have gone down a similar path, recovery can be extremely difficult, especially if they have difficulty with the social skills or lack social awareness of what they are entitled to (for example, social security). However, since her diagnosis, she appears to have found out what social benefits she is entitled to and has had access to a social worker.

Of higher functioning members, I also met Lawrie who wasn't diagnosed with Asperger's syndrome until he was 37. Unlike most other members of the group, Lawrie was in permanent employment. He worked with Queensland Rail, but had been in the same position that he had gained after leaving high school. His position involved very basic maintenance, mostly cleaning rolling stock. Lawrie said that many people with whom he entered work with in Queensland Rail had since either moved up into superior positions or had moved on to more superior positions elsewhere. Perhaps he had never been considered for more superior positions because he may have been seen as lacking the necessary social skills.

There was another member of the group who had been diagnosed late in life, John, who was studying Music Therapy at the University of Queensland. He wasn't diagnosed until he was 42! At 20, I had felt that my diagnosis came late enough, but to reinvent oneself at this kind of age must have been quite difficult. However, John appeared to be very relaxed and rather optimistic, more so than he said he ever was before his diagnosis. Like myself, a diagnosis had made a positive difference to his life.

My experience of meeting other young adults with Asperger's syndrome helped me realise that individual personalities and backgrounds of people with Asperger's syndrome are very different. Also, the way that other people with Asperger's syndrome respond to their backgrounds/surroundings is very different. There was a wide range of personalities and interests among the members of Garry's Young Adults Group. Most of all, I enjoyed the experience of being with a group of Australian adults with Asperger's syndrome to whom I felt I could relate really well to. They also felt that they could relate well to me in return.

A.S.S.

Three years later, I visited Canada to meet Tara Kimberley Torme. Tara was waiting for me at Vancouver International Airport. Almost immediately, I recognised her from the photograph she had sent me and she recognised me. Just like I had experienced when meeting Garry in person for the first time, we felt that we had known each other for years! People with Asperger's syndrome, including myself, often feel so misunderstood by people around us. But I find that when we get the opportunity to meet others with the condition who we feel can understand us, we feel as though we have known each other for years even if we have never previously met in person.

Like Garry, Tara was also starting up a social group for people with Asperger's syndrome in Vancouver when I visited. She decided to start such a group after a disagreement with a local Autistic society over their interpretation of Asperger's syndrome as a disability and after finding that there wasn't a support group for young adults with Asperger's syndrome in Vancouver. The purpose of the Asperger's Social and Support Group (A.S.S.) that Tara was promoting through a newsletter was to provide a place where adults with Asperger's syndrome could meet regularly and where they could feel understood, as well as taking part in social activities such as coffee meets, going bowling and so on. I really liked this concept, as it sounded like a good way of meeting other people with Asperger's syndrome.

A.S.S. coffee meets took place at a local independent café called 'The Grind'. This was a really good place to have an Asperger's social meeting, as it was located on the outskirts of Vancouver in a rather quiet neighbourhood and wasn't very busy. I usually prefer the atmosphere of a small coffee shop which is often quiet opposed to a pub, which can sometimes get noisy if people have had a bit too much to drink.

Of other A.S.S. members, I met Leslie, who was a really nice person, although he appeared to talk continuously, often having difficulty being able to recognise when others had perhaps had enough of what he was talking about. From what he said, gaps in his high-school education had limited what he could do as an adult and he had lived off disability benefits for much of his adult life. Another person I met was Tim, who was very much the opposite of Leslie, very quiet. In most situations, Tim appeared to be rather shy, but also liked to perform comedy on stage in his spare time. On stage, he was a completely different person, with the comedy providing a mask for his shyness. What I liked about the A.S.S. coffee meet was the wide range of Asperger's syndrome personalities of people with Asperger's syndrome that I met. Someone else who was again very different was Natalie, who was rather confident and also very fitness-orientated.

Aspies united!

My visits to Australia and Canada to meet Garry and Tara were like Asperger's syndrome cultural exchanges. Garry has since come to visit me in the UK and Tara intends to sometime in the not too distant future. From my experience with Garry and Tara and their Asperger's syndrome groups, I found out more about Asperger's syndrome personalities, in particular that all individuals who have the condition are different in terms of personality.

If it weren't for my Asperger's syndrome diagnosis, I wouldn't have met Garry or Tara and probably might not even have travelled. Our experiences of each other's company shows how Asperger's syndrome diagnosis can make a difference to people's lives in terms of friendships that we wouldn't have otherwise had.

15

Aspie of Intrigue:
My Cruise Experience

Occasionally, my Aspie traits are recognised by people who don't know that I have the condition. When this happens, I often feel it necessary to tell the person who notices that I have Asperger's syndrome. A notable situation where this occurred was when I took a cruise to Alaska, where I also discovered a different side of myself.

Radiance of the Seas

My cruise to Alaska was on board Royal Caribbean's Radiance of the Seas. I had never been on a cruise before, but little was I to know I was about to encounter a life-changing experience. My immediate impression of Radiance of the Seas was that it was a floating Las Vegas.

When I booked the cruise, I was given an option of the age range with whom I would like to have dinner. I picked the 19 to 26 option, as it may have been fun to be with some Americans around my age and I would be a Brit among Americans. That night, I was placed at a table with a girl from Los Angeles, Andrea, who was quite near my age and also came on a singles package. I wasn't quite sure what the intention of this placing was, but I was not used to having a three-course meal with a female. I felt a little nervous at first as I didn't have a clue how to act around females, but when Andrea saw that I wasn't coming on to her she felt comfortable talking to me. We found out that we lived in completely different worlds. She was a party planner based in Hollywood who organised parties for movie stars and here was I, the Aspie librarian from one of the quieter parts of England.

We were two completely different personalities. In contrast to me, Andrea appeared very active and outgoing and had even appeared on *Russian Roulette*, a gameshow on American television, not long before the cruise. Like me, she was hoping to be at a table with other people her age. After dinner, Andrea asked me if I was going to go to the singles meeting place at the nightclub on the top deck.

Karaoke

When we went up, we saw that one of the activities was karaoke, where there were some other young people and families. However, being the only non-American in the room at the time, I got a huge cheer after the host asked me to tell everyone who I was and where I was from. At first I was frightened to get up on stage, but when the hosts needed some requests, one of the audience members asked if the guy from England would sing because she liked English accents. I got up and the host found a song for me, 'Gigolo' by David Lee Roth.

After being on stage, I felt much more confident and had a look through the songs available and very quickly found one that I knew well and felt like singing – Don McLean's 'American Pie', at eight-and-a-half minutes, the longest karaoke song in history. As I knew the song so well, I felt very confident and could focus on the audience much more. I was really enjoying myself performing and the audience loved it! The next day was spent at sea, but there was plenty on board Radiance of the Seas to keep me occupied. The entire atmosphere on board made me feel much less nervous and much more relaxed and no-one would have thought that I had any real problems interacting with others.

A lot of other passengers had seen me the first night and were looking forward to see me up on stage again the next evening. This time, I sang Bruce Springsteen's 'Born in the USA'. Again, it was a great feeling being up on stage. The host, Elaine, said afterwards: "Never before have I heard that song performed in an English accent, you're the cutest!" That was the first time I had ever been called that by a young woman!

First football medal

In this environment, I felt so confident in myself that I found myself doing things that I hadn't done on shore for a long time, including working out in the gym, going swimming and playing football. The three-on-three football tournament was probably the highlight. I was placed in a team with two 18-year-old American boys. Our first game was against a team of two brothers and a sister. I had almost forgotten how to kick a ball as it was so long since I last played the game, but once I got a touch and completed a pass, I knew I could still kick it. I remembered how, when I played at school, if you don't let your opponents play by closing them down, you could win possession and catch them on the counter attack. Our opponents took an early lead, but we came back from behind to win. My two team mates were more comfortable on the ball than I was, but I kept the pressure on the opponents and it worked well.

We finished as runners-up in the competition, although I was just surprised at getting beyond the first game! After the final, we were given medals. This was the first time that I had ever won a football medal. I missed out on this at school and I used to get really frustrated when my younger brother's bedroom used to get filled with trophies and medals and I had nothing. However, after all those years, I finally won my first football medal off the coast of Alaska of all places!

Food preferences

For the remainder of my cruise, I was placed at a table with different passengers, who made me feel very welcome. It was a couple from Dallas, Stan and Mary-Anne that introduced me to the others, including Mike and Anna from Boston and John and Eliana from Vancouver. After being introduced, I felt so comfortable in being able to make conversation.

My table friends noticed that I stuck with the steak option for my main course and ice cream for desert, and said that they had become used to it! Often, I find myself sticking to a particular food option after I become used to it, rather than varying what I eat. At this point, I felt it necessary to tell my table friends that I had Asperger's syndrome. As a teacher, Anna had taught pupils with special needs, including Asperger's syndrome pupils. She was surprised when I told her that I had the condition, saying that she would never have noticed. In return I said that such traits probably weren't noticeable in such a party atmosphere. Anna said that I was the first adult with the condition that she had ever met and that it helped her to understand how people with the condition can lead fulfilling lives.

Both Anna and Mike had very caring sides to them, Mike could relate to how developmental disabilities affect families, as he had a brother who has dyslexia. Stan and Mary-Anne, who both worked in healthcare, were also interested to hear about it and could relate well with much of what I said about my upbringing, as they had a son with ADHD.

Big hit on board?

Back home in England, I tend to lead a very quiet life, but on board Radiance of the Seas, the whole environment made me a very different person for a week. I felt so much more comfortable interacting with others than I normally do and it helped when I found that most of the other passengers were keen to get to know me, having seen me at different events on board and on shore. I got on with many different people as well as my dinner friends and people I met playing football and at karaoke. I think it was fair to say that I was a big hit on board Radiance of the Seas! The dinner evenings really turned out to be the highlight of the cruise. We were all sat together at a table courtesy of a rearrangement, but it worked out really well. Looking back it might have been even better had we been together from the first night. I really felt as though I fitted in with the Americans as they were all so open and felt comfortable talking about personal issues such as autism.

At the last evening of karaoke, I decided to give a good send-off by singing my favourite track, 'Born in the USA', again. My table friends all came up to see me, and on stage, I thanked them for making my cruise experience so wonderful. At the end of the evening, the cruise staff told me how much I would be missed on board Radiance of the Seas. Some other passengers also asked if they could have their photograph taken with me, saying that I had been such an inspiration! As the ship docked in Vancouver on the last morning, I said goodbye to all the people who I had met, wishing them a safe journey home. In return, I thanked both them and the crew on board Radiance of the Seas for their hospitality. I will forever feel that this whole experience added a new dimension to my personality.

16

A Reflection:
How Asperger's Syndrome Has Changed My Life

Being diagnosed with Asperger's syndrome has changed my life in many ways. At school, I was bullied by other people who got bullied and as a teenager, I felt I missed out on so much socially. Knowing that I have Asperger's syndrome has made me more assertive as to who I am. Since my diagnosis, I have learned more about myself that I ever previously knew and my ambitions and general outlook on life changed. Most importantly, I have learned not to live up to anybody's expectations other than my own.

For the first 19 years of my life, I felt as if I was someone who didn't exist. I found myself having to live up to the standards and expectations of others, particularly in terms of social behaviour. Since being diagnosed, however, I find that when others know that I have Asperger's syndrome, they are much more tolerant of me than they were during the years where I had to try and pretend to be normal, something that I am not. Such tolerance has strengthened my relationships with my family.

To the casual observer, I may not appear to have had the most successful of lives. I have never married or even been in a relationship, never owned a home and I am yet to establish myself in a long-term career (although I am not far off). However, in my own right, I feel as though I have been successful in a more unconventional way, in the sense that I have been able to make a difference to the lives of other people with Asperger's syndrome. Through my experience and upbringing of undiagnosed Asperger's syndrome, I am able to make others aware of Asperger's syndrome as well as helping other people with the condition not having to go through what I had to when younger.

The assertiveness and self-confidence that I have developed since my diagnosis has enabled me to do public speaking. Public speaking is a great way for me to express myself as well as informing others about Asperger's syndrome. As I have Asperger's syndrome, when it is coming from me, I feel that it is my own expression. But at the same time, it is helping others understand it. The Asperger's syndrome self-advocacy I have developed through public speaking has enabled me to become more open about issues in my life with others, including being able to write this book. An issue that I sometimes talk about at my speaking engagements is a cure for Asperger's syndrome, something that has been debated on autism e-mailing lists. Personally, I would not accept a cure for Asperger's syndrome if one became available, as I consider it to be the most important characteristic of who I am, rather than a label. Most of all, I wouldn't want to go back to my pre-diagnosis days.

Too many decisions about my life, I felt, were made by others prior to diagnosis. Knowing that I have Asperger's syndrome, however, has enabled me to make my own personal analysis of what I consider to be my strengths and weaknesses. Knowing my strengths and weaknesses has helped me to reinvent myself in a way so that NT's (Neuro Typicals, or people without autism) can tolerate me. At the same time though, I can keep my Asperger's traits, as they can be strengths, especially my memory and eye for detail. From my analysis, I have found that I am much more comfortable with routine and predictability than I am with pressure. Roles in which I feel most comfortable involve order and structure (for example, admin/clerical duties) rather than high-pressured environments (for example, sales). Such tasks that include much repetitiveness may seem rather mundane to some, but to me such tasks are reassuring. Other people may enjoy the challenge and excitement of a high-pressure environment, whereas I would probably experience high levels of anxiety due the unpredictability of such an environment, which would result in stress.

To many people around me, the quiet and often sheltered lifestyle that I tend to lead might appear as rather boring and very lonely. But the way I see it, many NT's need to have a wide circle of friends, a family or to be in a relationship to be happy. Many NT's, I find, need to have something to gossip about, which is why soap operas and reality TV shows such as *Big Brother* exist along with celebrity magazines such as *Hello*. Meanwhile, I am able to amuse myself with lone interests such as reading, making model buildings and so on.

Whereas I left school with no friends or contacts, my brother and cousins had many friends at school, some of whom they still see regularly. My brother still plays Sunday league football with people whom he went to school with. I have seen very little of people that I knew at school and in many cases, I wouldn't recognise people that knew me at school if I passed them in the street. Meanwhile, my parents and my brother and sister have subscribed to 'Friends Reunited', the website that puts people in touch with their former school friends. I have no intention of joining such a service. Some people may consider their school days to be 'the best days of their lives', but to me, they were some of the most difficult. At school, I missed out on many social activities, such as playing football with other people my age regularly, being in rock bands with other people my age and so on. When an undergraduate student at university, I often felt that I wasn't wanted or felt out of place around career-minded individuals with no time for the likes of myself. As I feel that I missed out on so much socially when younger, this has motivated me to make up for it in later life, such as pursuing postgraduate study and travelling overseas to meet new friends.

Whereas I haven't seen anybody with whom I did my undergraduate degree with at the University of Teesside, I still see some of my Masters' colleagues occasionally. Personally though, the best thing that has happened to me since my diagnosis is that it has enabled me to meet other people with Asperger's syndrome, as well as taking me to places such as Australia and Canada, that I probably wouldn't have otherwise seen. Since subscribing to Autuniv-l, I have met other Aspies to whom I feel I can relate in terms of experience and share similar issues and concerns. Eventually, I developed the desire to go beyond the computer screen and meet other Aspies, including Garry and Tara, in person. In this way I feel that I have united myself and other Aspies around the world.

I feel that my Asperger's syndrome diagnosis has enabled me to lead a fulfilling life. From being the child who didn't have many friends, who got bullied and spent much of his spare time to himself in his room, I have gone on to share enjoyment and adventure with other Aspies. From bush walking in Australia to walking the glaciers of Alaska, and most of all, through the people I have met since diagnosis, I feel that I have more than made up for what I missed out on when younger, not to mention all the 'social corrections' and bullying that I had to put up with. Who knows whom I will meet and what adventures I will have next?

Further Resources

The central resource for information and support concerning Asperger's syndrome in the UK is the National Autistic Society that publishes a newsletter, Asperger United, by and for people with Asperger's.

The National Autistic Society
393 City Road, London, EC1V 1NG, UK
Tel: +44 (0)20 7833 2299
Fax: +44 (0)20 7833 9666
Email: nas@nas.org.uk
Website: http://www.oneworld.org/autism_uk/

The Society runs specialist centres for diagnosis of autism and Asperger's syndrome:

The Centre for Social & Communication Disorders
Elliot House, 113 Masons Hill, Bromley, Kent, BR2 9HT, UK
Tel: + 44 (0)20 8466 0098
Fax: + 44 (0)20 8466 0118
email: elliot.house@nas.org.uk

EarlyBird Centre
3 Victoria Crescent West, Barnsley, South Yorkshire, S75 2AE, UK
Tel: +44 (0)1226 779218
Fax: +44 (0)1266 771014
email: earlybird@nas.org.uk

Help! Programme
Church House, Church Road, Filton, Bristol, BS34 7BD, UK
Tel: +44 (0)117 974 8411
Fax: +44 (0)117 987 2576
email: help!@nas.org.uk

Prospects (Supported Employment)
Studio 8, The Ivories, 6-8 Northampton Street, London, N1 2HY, UK
Tel: +44 (0)20 7704 7450
Fax: +44 (0)20 7359 9440
email: prospects@nas.org.uk

A specialist further education college for people with Asperger's syndrome:
The INTERACT Centre
c/o Hanwell Community Centre, Westcott Crescent, London, W7 1PD, UK

Tel: 020 8575 0046
Fax: 020 8575 0046
Email: office@theinteractcentre.com

Online Asperger syndrome Information Support (OASIS)
http://www.udel.edu/bkirby/asperger/index.html

European Services for People with Autism
6 - 7 The Cloisters, Sunderland, Tyne & Wear, SR2 7BD, UK
Tel: 0191 510 2600

For information regarding the help available to people with disabilities when finding work:
http://www.direct.gov.uk/Audiences/DisabledPeople/Employment/fs/en